Decisions for Health

BOOK TWO

VIVIAN BERNSTEIN

STECK-VAUGHN
ELEMENTARY · SECONDARY · ADULT · LIBRARY

A Harcourt Company

www.steck-vaughn.com

About the Author

Vivian Bernstein has been a teacher in the New York City Public School System for a number of years. She received her Master of Arts degree from New York University. Bernstein is active with professional organizations in social studies, education, and reading. She gives presentations to school faculties and professional groups about content area reading. Bernstein is the author of *America's Story, World History and You, World Geography and You,* and *American Government.*

Acknowledgments

Unit 1 pp.2-3 © Tony Freeman/PhotoEdit; p.4 © Tony Freeman/PhotoEdit; p.5 © R. Becker/Custom Medical Stock Photo; p.7 © Tony Freeman/PhotoEdit; p.8 © Jeffry Myers/Stock Boston; p.11 © Robert Brenner/PhotoEdit; p.15 © J. Berndt/Stock Boston; p.16 © Myrleen Ferguson/PhotoEdit; p.22 © Spencer Grant/Photo Researchers; p.24 © Michael Newman/PhotoEdit; p.27 © Myrleen Ferguson/PhotoEdit; p.30 © Tony Freeman/PhotoEdit. Unit 2 pp.34-35 © Myrleen Ferguson/PhotoEdit; p.36 © Tony Freeman/PhotoEdit; p.37 © Robert Brenner/PhotoEdit; p.38 © Tony Freeman/PhotoEdit; p.39 © Lawrence Migdale/Photo Researchers; p.42 © Spencer Grant/Stock Boston; p.43 © Elizabeth Crews/Stock Boston; p.44 © Peter Menzel/Stock Boston; p.45 © Mary Kate Denny/PhotoEdit; p.49 © Bill Bachman/Photo Researchers; p.50 © Tony Freeman/PhotoEdit; p.51 © Barbara Rios/Photo Researchers; p.52 © Barbara Rios/Photo Researchers; p.53 © Tony Freeman/PhotoEdit; p.56 (egg) © Richard Rawlins/Custom Medical Stock Photo, (sperm) © J.L. Carson/Custom Medical Stock Photo; p.58 © Billy Barnes/Stock Boston; p.59 © Nancy Durrell McKenna/Photo Researchers; p.60 © Jeffry Myers/Stock Boston; p.61 © Myrleen Ferguson/PhotoEdit; p.64 © Robert Brenner/PhotoEdit; p.65 © Ulrike Welsch/PhotoEdit; p.66 © Gale Zucker/Stock Boston; p.67 © Myrleen Ferguson/PhotoEdit; p.68 © Kathy Sloane/Photo Researchers; p.69 © Tony Freeman/PhotoEdit. Unit 3 pp.72-73 © Tony Freeman/PhotoEdit; p.74 © Focus On Sports; p.75 © Tony Freeman/PhotoEdit; p.76 © Siu Biomed Comm/Custom Medical Stock Photo; p.77 © Charles Gatewood/Stock Boston; p.78 © Tom Prettyman/PhotoEdit; p.79 © Michael Weisbrot/Stock Boston; p.80 © Tony Freeman/PhotoEdit; p.83 © D.Cantwell/Custom Medical Stock Photo; p.84 © Frank Siteman/Stock Boston; p.85 © Charles Gatewood/Stock Boston; p.86 © Tony Freeman/PhotoEdit; p.87 © Elizabeth Zuckerman/PhotoEdit; p.88 © Laimute Druskis/Stock Boston; p.89 © Bob Daemmrich/Stock Boston; p.92 © Mary Kate Denny/PhotoEdit; p.93 © Tony Freeman/PhotoEdit; p.94 © Robert Brenner/PhotoEdit; p.95 © Mary Kate Denny/PhotoEdit; p.96 © Jeffrey Myers/Stock Boston; p.99 © Charles Gatewood/Stock Boston; p.100 © Custom Medical Stock Photo; p.101 © Custom Medical Stock Photo; p.102 © Elizabeth Zuckerman/PhotoEdit. Unit 4 pp.106-107 © Biomedical Communications/Photo Researchers; p.108 © Bernard Peirre Wolff/Photo Researchers; p.109 © Mary Kate Denny/PhotoEdit; p.110 © Custom Medical Stock Photo; p.111 © L. Drukskis/Stock Boston; p.115 Center For Disease Control; p.116 ©Tim Barnwell/Stock Boston; p.118 © Thomas Bowman/PhotoEdit; p.119 © National Medical Slide/Custom Medical Stock Photo; p.121 © Robert Brenner/PhotoEdit; p.125 (healthy) © Custom Medical Stock Photo; p.125 (diseased) ©Roseman/Custom Medical Stock Photo; p.126 © Custom Medical Stock Photo; p.127 © Scott Camazine/Photo Researchers; p.128 © Bob Daemmrich/Stock Boston; p.131 © Steve Skjold/PhotoEdit; p.132 © Custom Medical Stock Photo; p.133 © Custom Medical Stock Photo; p.137 © Blair Seitz/Photo Researchers; p.138 © L. Steinmark/Custom Medical Stock Photo; p.139 © Custom Medical Stock Photo; p.140 © Custom Medical Stock Photo.

Consultants:

Lori A. Hagen: Ms. Hagen is a special education teacher in Albuquerque, New Mexico.

Elnora P. Mendías, MS, RN, CFNP: Ms. Mendías is a doctoral candidate at The University of Texas at Austin School of Nursing.

Credits:

Executive Editor: Diane Sharpe

Project Editor: Patricia Reyna

Designer: John J. Harrison

Photo Editor: Margie Foster

Production: Howard Adkins Communications, Sandra Schmitt

Illustrations: Accurate Art, Inc.

ISBN 0-8114-3301-3

Contents

To the Reader

Your body is an amazing machine. Hundreds of parts work together for you every minute of the day. Your heart beats, your brain thinks, and your ears hear. To work well your body needs good care. It needs exercise, sleep, and a healthy diet.

You can protect your body. You can protect it with a diet that is low in fat. You can build a strong heart by exercising at least three times a week. By getting along with your family and friends, you also protect your health. You can protect your body with good health habits that help you avoid disease.

You can also harm your body and ruin your health. Smoking cigarettes damages your heart and lungs. You can destroy your health with alcohol and drug abuse. Risk behaviors can lead to AIDS. You can also harm yourself with poor health habits that lead to other diseases.

As you read *Decisions for Health, Book Two*, you will learn how to protect your body. You will learn how to keep your body strong. You will learn how to avoid harmful behaviors. You will learn many good health habits that will protect you from drug abuse and disease. By making good health habits part of your life, you can enjoy many years of good health.

UNIT 1

Growth and Development

Imagine being a member of a band. To be a great band, all the players and their instruments must work together. Like the band the parts of your body must work together so you can be healthy.

The parts of your body depend on each other. Strong bones and muscles allow you to move easily. Exercise makes your heart stronger. A strong, healthy heart can pump blood easily to every part of the body.

Have You Ever Wondered?

▼ Your bones cannot move without your muscles. How do muscles move bones?
▼ Your body has red blood cells and white blood cells. Why does it need both?
▼ You can breathe with your nose and with your mouth. It is healthier to breathe with your nose. Why?

As you read this unit, think of ways you can keep the parts of your body healthy so they can work together for you.

2

Your Cells, Bones, and Muscles

Think About as You Read

- **How do bones and muscles help you move?**
- **How can you have good posture?**
- **How can you build strong bones and muscles?**

Your body can move in many ways. It moves because you have bones and muscles.

Your body is always moving. It moves when you run and jump. It also moves when you turn over while you sleep. Your body can move because you have bones and muscles.

Millions of Cells

Cells are very tiny living things. All plants and animals are made of cells. You cannot see the cells of your body because the cells are too small. Every cell of the body must have food and **oxygen**.

The body has many kinds of cells. Some of the different cells are the blood cells, skin cells, and muscle cells. Large groups of cells form **organs** inside your body. Your heart, brain, and stomach are three organs. Groups of organs work together to form the body's **systems**.

Your Bones

Your body has more than 200 bones. The bones help you in four ways. First, your bones keep all of the other parts of your body in place so you can stand and sit. Second, your bones work with your muscles to help you move. Third, blood cells are made inside your bones. Fourth, your bones protect the organs inside your body. For example, your ribs protect your heart.

Oxygen is a gas that has no color or smell.

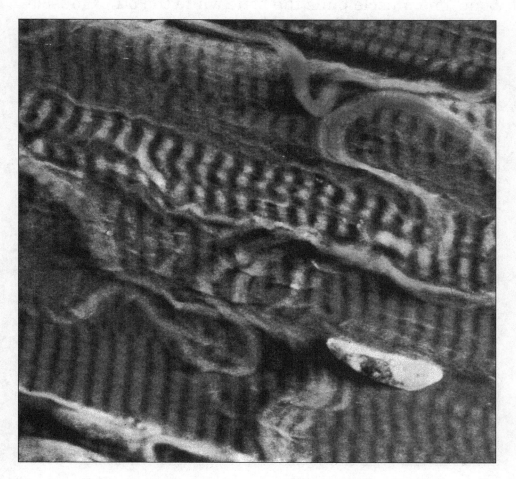

These are muscle cells as seen through a microscope.

Your body has three kinds of bones. You have long bones in your arms and legs. You have short bones in your hands, fingers, and spine. Flat bones protect your brain. The ribs around your heart are also flat bones.

Your bones fit together at **joints**. Some joints help you move. Your arms, legs, toes, and neck have joints so they can move. The bones that protect your brain and your heart have joints that do not move.

Your Muscles

Your body has more than 600 muscles. You have muscles all over your body. Skin covers your muscles. Small muscles allow you to move your eyes, lips, and tongue. Large muscles allow you to move your arms and legs.

Your body has two types of muscles. **Voluntary muscles** allow you to move. You can control your voluntary muscles. They are attached to the arms, legs, and spine. They are also attached to the other bones that move. Voluntary muscles work in pairs. To move a bone, one muscle pulls the bone while the other muscle relaxes.

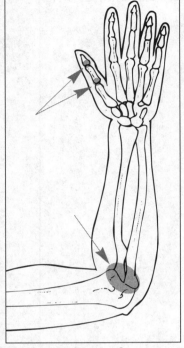

The bones fit together at joints. The arrows show a joint at the elbow and two joints in the thumb.

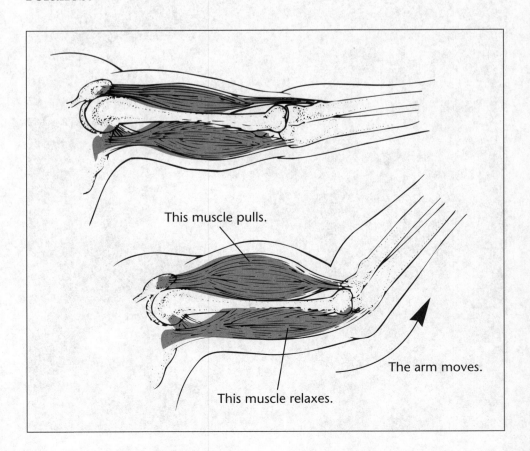

This muscle pulls.

The arm moves.

This muscle relaxes.

Muscles relax and pull to make your arm move.

You can stand and move because you have bones and muscles.

Involuntary muscles control your heart and your breathing. They keep your stomach working. Your brain sends messages to these muscles. With these messages the muscles can work on their own. These muscles keep working even while you sleep.

Taking Care of Your Bones and Muscles

Your **posture** is the way you carry your body when you sit, stand, and walk. You must use your bones and muscles to stand and sit correctly.

Why do you need good posture? Good posture helps your appearance. It also helps your bones and muscles grow the way they should. Also, good posture keeps your organs in their correct places inside your body.

There are three causes of poor posture. The first is poor standing and sitting habits. Many people do not work at having good standing and sitting habits. The lack of strong muscles in your back and stomach area is the second cause. The third cause is a health problem called **scoliosis**. Scoliosis is an unhealthy curving of the spine. Your school nurse or doctor can check your back for scoliosis during a checkup. It should be treated when it is found in teen-agers. Scoliosis can cause other health problems.

You can have good posture. Practice standing and sitting correctly. Do exercises to make the muscles in your back and around your stomach stronger.

To build strong bones and muscles, exercise at least three times a week. Walk, run, jog, or play tennis. Jumping rope and lifting weights also make your bones and muscles stronger. Stretching exercises help arms and legs bend and move easily. As you grow older, you should continue to do stretching exercises as well as exercises to build your bones and muscles.

Lifting objects correctly is a way to care for your back. Always lift objects by bending at your knees. Keep your back straight.

Osteoporosis is a bone disease that can affect older adults. To protect yourself from this disease, eat enough foods with **calcium**. Milk, cheese, and dark green vegetables have lots of calcium. Do exercises that build strong bones.

You use your bones and muscles to move. You must take care of them by having good posture habits. Eat foods with calcium every day and exercise at least three times a week. Caring for your bones and muscles will help you have a healthy body.

Calcium is a mineral that the body needs for strong bones and teeth.

Milk, cheese, and dark green vegetables are rich in calcium. Eat them to have healthy bones.

Vocabulary—Matching

Match the vocabulary word in **Group B** with its definition from **Group A**. Write the letter of the correct answer on the line.

Group A

Group B

_____ 1. These are formed by large groups of cells.

a. posture

_____ 2. This is the way you carry your body when you sit, stand, and move.

b. systems

c. involuntary

_____ 3. This is found in milk, cheese, and dark green vegetables.

d. organs

e. calcium

_____ 4. These are formed by groups of organs that work together.

_____ 5. These muscles control your heart and your breathing.

Comprehension—Write the Answer

Write an answer in a complete sentence to each question. The first one is done for you.

1. Why can't you see the cells in your body?

   You can't see the cells in your body because they are so small.

2. Which bones protect your heart?

   _____

   _____

3. What is scoliosis?

   _____

   _____

4. How often should you exercise to build strong bones and muscles?

_____

_____

5. How do voluntary muscles work?

_____

_____

Critical Thinking—Categories

Read the words in each group. Decide how they are alike. Find the best title in the box for each group. Write the title on the line beside each group.

involuntary muscles	good posture
cells	bones

1. found in all living things _____
   too small to see
   need food and oxygen

2. can be long, short, or flat_____
   help you move
   protect your organs

3. control your heart and breathing _____
   keep your stomach working
   work even while you are sleeping

4. helps your appearance _____
   keeps your organs in the correct places
   helps your bones and muscles grow correctly

The Digestive and Circulatory Systems

Think About as You Read

- What happens to food in the digestive system?
- How does blood move through your body?
- How can you care for your digestive and circulatory systems?

Fruits and vegetables are healthy foods. They have many nutrients that your body needs.

Every cell in your body must have oxygen. Every cell also needs **nutrients** from the food you eat. Your body breaks down food so your cells can get nutrients. Your blood carries the nutrients and oxygen to every cell of the body.

Nutrients are substances in food that the body needs for health and life.

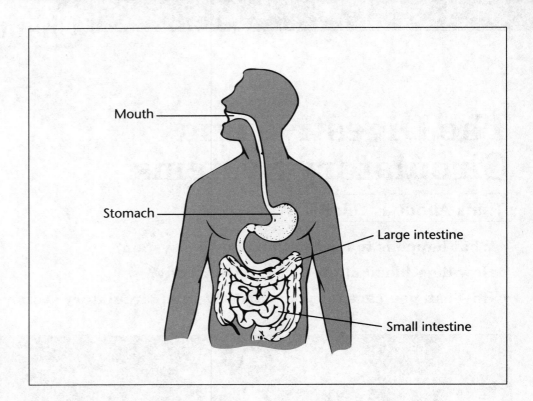

Mouth

Stomach

Large intestine

Small intestine

The organs of the digestive system break down food so it can be used by your cells.

The Work of the Digestive System

The food that you eat must be changed so its nutrients can be used by the body. Your body has a group of organs that breaks down food so it can be used by the body. These organs form your **digestive system**.

Digestion begins in the mouth. Your teeth chew food into small pieces. As you chew, **enzymes** in your mouth begin to break down the food.

Food passes from the mouth through a long tube and enters your stomach. Muscles and enzymes in the stomach break down the food further. After food is digested by the stomach, it then passes into the **small intestine**.

The small intestine finishes most of the job of digestion. More enzymes break down the food. The digested food is now ready to leave the small intestine. This digested food looks like thin soup. Now the body's cells can use the digested food.

Digested food passes through the walls of the small intestine into the blood. Then your blood carries nutrients from the digested food to every cell.

Digestion is the way the body breaks down your food into nutrients the body can use.

Enzymes are chemicals made by the body and used to break down food.

Digestion cannot break down some foods, like fruit skins. Foods that cannot be digested become solid waste. The **large intestine** stores solid waste until the solid waste leaves the body.

The Circulatory System

The **circulatory system** has three parts. The three parts are the heart, the blood, and the **blood vessels**. **Arteries**, **veins**, and **capillaries** are the three types of blood vessels in the body.

The job of the circulatory system is to bring food and oxygen to every part of the body. To do this job, the heart pumps blood. Then blood vessels carry blood to every cell of the body. Then other blood vessels carry blood back to the heart. This happens thousands of times each day. The heart never stops pumping while a person is alive.

Blood vessels are the different kinds of tubes that carry blood throughout the body.

Arteries are blood vessels that carry blood away from the heart to other parts of the body.

Veins are blood vessels that carry blood from other parts of the body back to the heart.

Capillaries are very tiny blood vessels that connect arteries and veins. Capillaries carry blood, oxygen, and nutrients to the body cells.

The Circulatory System

vein

lungs

artery

heart

Your heart pumps all the time. Blood vessels carry blood to every cell in your body.

13

How Blood Moves Through the Body

Your circulatory system moves your blood throughout your body.

1. The right side of the heart pumps blood with **carbon dioxide** to the lungs.
2. Blood gets oxygen and loses carbon dioxide at the lungs.
3. Blood leaves the lungs and is pumped to the left side of the heart.
4. The left side of the heart pumps blood into the arteries. The arteries divide into smaller blood vessels called capillaries. The capillaries carry blood to the body cells.
5. Capillaries bring oxygen and nutrients to the body cells. Capillaries pick up carbon dioxide and waste.
6. Capillaries join to form larger blood vessels called veins. Veins carry carbon dioxide to the right side of the heart.

When cells use nutrients and oxygen, they make a gas called **carbon dioxide**. Carbon dioxide leaves the body when you breathe out.

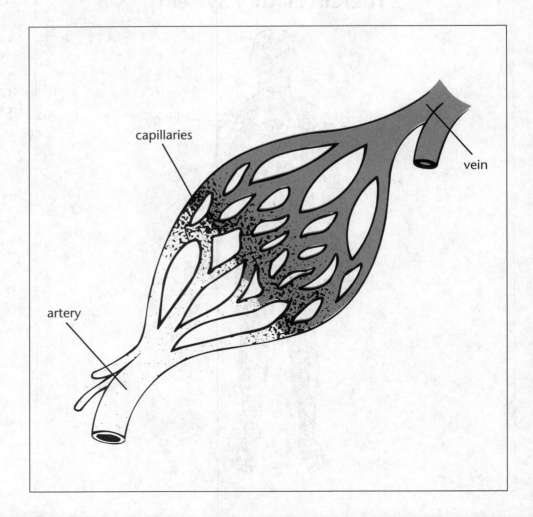

capillaries

vein

artery

Arteries, capillaries, and veins are the three kinds of blood vessels.

14

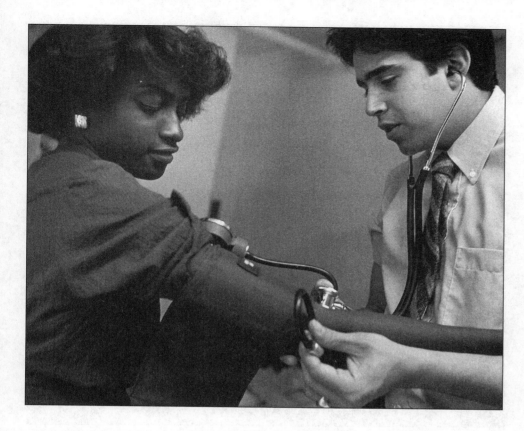

Your doctor should check your blood pressure when you have a checkup.

Your Blood and Your Blood Pressure

Your blood has red blood cells and white blood cells. Both kinds of blood cells are made inside your bones. You have more red blood cells than white blood cells. The red blood cells carry oxygen. The white blood cells help your body fight germs. You would be sick most of the time if you did not have white blood cells.

Your **blood pressure** is the force of your blood as it moves against the walls of the arteries or the heart. The arteries can stretch to become larger or smaller. This helps the blood flow through the arteries.

Some people have a health problem called high blood pressure. High blood pressure occurs for many reasons. People with high blood pressure have overworked hearts. High blood pressure can cause tiny blood vessels to burst. This can damage body organs, such as the brain. High blood pressure can also lead to heart disease or other body organ diseases. Your doctor should check your blood pressure when you have a checkup. A healthy diet, exercise, and medicine can help treat high blood pressure.

15

To have a healthy heart, exercise at least three times a week. Eat less fat and salt.

Caring for Your Digestive and Circulatory Systems

Follow these five rules to keep your systems healthy.

1. Exercise at least three times a week. Exercise makes your heart and arteries stronger. It helps lower your blood pressure.
2. Do not smoke or use drugs in ways that are not correct. Do not drink alcohol.
3. Control your weight. Do not eat more food than you need. Your heart must work much harder if you are overweight.
4. Eat a healthy diet. Eat many fruits and vegetables. Your diet should be low in fat and salt. Eat less fried food, egg yolks, and red meat. Drink skim milk instead of whole milk.
5. See your doctor for regular checkups. If you have high blood pressure, it should be treated.

Take care of your body's systems. Caring for your body's systems will help you have a healthy body.

Vocabulary—Find the Meaning

On the line write the word or words that best complete each sentence.

1. The _____ system is the group of organs that break down food so it can be used by the body.

   circulatory   **digestive**   **bone**

2. The gas made by cells when they use nutrients and oxygen is

   _____ .

   small intestine   **blood**   **carbon dioxide**

3. The _____ carry blood away from the heart.

   arteries   **enzymes**   **nutrients**

4. The _____ stores solid waste.

   capillary   **large intestine**   **heart**

5. The chemicals in the body that help break down food are

   _____ .

   enzymes   **wastes**   **oxygen**

Comprehension—Writing About Health

Answer the following question in complete sentences.

What are three things you can do to care for your digestive and circulatory systems?

_____

_____

_____

_____

An **analogy** compares two pairs of words. The words in the first pair are alike in the same way as the words in the second pair. For example, **green** is to **grass** as **blue** is to **sky**. Use a word or words in the box to finish each sentence. The first one is done for you.

nutrients	veins	circulatory system	large intestine
solid wastes	mouth	white blood cells	exercise

1. The small intestine is to finishing digestion as the __mouth__ is to beginning digestion.

2. The digestive system is to food as the _____ is to blood.

3. Red blood cells are to carrying oxygen as _____ are to fighting germs.

4. Oxygen is to air as _____ are to food.

5. Carbon dioxide is to the circulatory system as _____ are to the digestive system.

6. Arteries are to carrying blood away from the heart as

   _____ are to carrying blood back to the heart.

7. A healthy diet is to controlling your weight as _____ is to building a strong heart and arteries.

8. The small intestine is to digested food as the _____ is to solid waste.

The Respiratory and Urinary Systems

Think About as You Read

- **How does your body take in oxygen?**
- **How do the kidneys clean the blood?**
- **How can diet and exercise help your systems?**

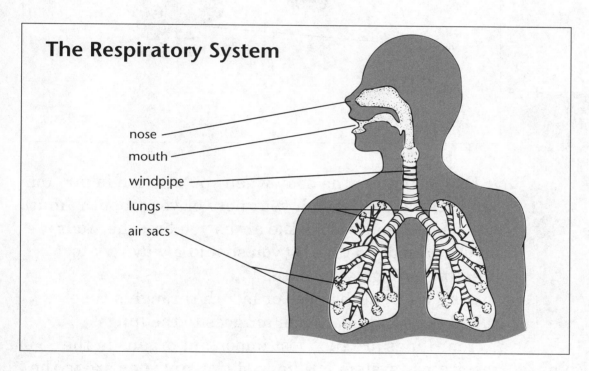

The Respiratory System

nose
mouth
windpipe
lungs
air sacs

Your respiratory system is a group of organs that brings oxygen into your body.

Every cell in your body needs oxygen. It is the job of your **respiratory system** to bring oxygen into your body. As your blood carries nutrients and oxygen to the cells, wastes are formed. It is the job of your **urinary system** to clean your blood by removing liquid waste.

Your **respiratory system** takes in oxygen and gives off carbon dioxide.

How Does the Respiratory System Work?

Your respiratory system is the group of organs that brings oxygen into the body. This system also removes carbon dioxide waste from the body.

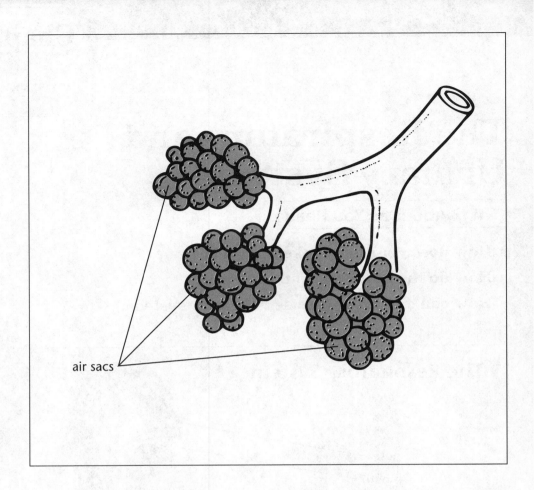

air sacs

Millions of tiny air sacs are in your lungs. Oxygen in the air sacs goes into your blood.

Air sacs are tiny bags of air in the lungs that are surrounded by blood vessels.

Oxygen enters the body when you breathe in air. You can breathe air through your nose or your mouth. Your nose cleans and warms the air as you breathe. Your mouth cannot do this. So you should always try to breathe through your nose.

Air goes from the nose or mouth through a tube called the windpipe. Then air goes to the lungs.

Your lungs are the most important organs in the respiratory system. Millions of tiny **air sacs** are in the lungs. Tiny blood vessels surround each air sac. Oxygen from the air goes into the air sacs. The heart pumps blood to the lungs. Oxygen in the air sacs goes into the blood at the lungs. Then blood with oxygen leaves the lungs and goes back to the heart. Your heart pumps this blood to every part of the body.

You know that the veins carry blood with carbon dioxide waste back to the heart. The heart pumps this blood to the lungs. The blood gets rid of carbon dioxide in the lungs. Carbon dioxide leaves the lungs when you breathe out. Your respiratory system does this job thousands of times each day.

This is how the respiratory system works.

1. You breathe in air through the nose or mouth.
2. Air goes into the windpipe.
3. The windpipe carries air to the lungs.
4. In the lungs, oxygen from the air goes into the blood. Blood is pumped by the heart to all parts of the body.
5. Blood loses carbon dioxide in the lungs.
6. Carbon dioxide leaves the lungs when you breathe out air.

How to Care for Your Respiratory System

You should follow these six rules to take care of your respiratory system.

1. Do not smoke. Smoking causes lung disease.
2. Try to avoid breathing **polluted** air. Do not sit in areas of restaurants and airplanes that allow smoking. Avoid breathing dirty gases given off by cars, buses, and trucks.

Polluted describes something that is dirty and unhealthy.

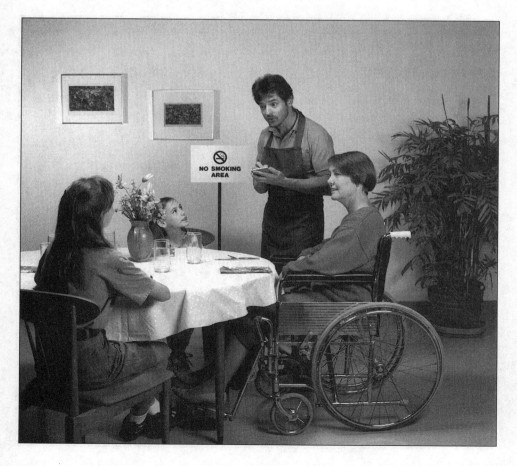

Many restaurants have areas that do not allow smoking.

3. Eat healthy foods and get enough sleep.
4. Exercise. Exercising makes your lungs strong.
5. See your doctor for regular checkups. Your doctor will listen to your lungs to make sure they are healthy.
6. Wear a face mask if you must be near dangerous gases or **asbestos**. You can badly damage your lungs by breathing dangerous gases or asbestos.

Removing Wastes from the Body

Your body makes wastes as it uses nutrients and oxygen. The body must get rid of these wastes in order to be healthy. Your body has four ways to get rid of wastes.

1. You breathe out carbon dioxide waste from your lungs.
2. You remove **perspiration** through your skin when you sweat.
3. Your large intestine removes solid waste left by the foods you cannot digest.
4. Liquid waste is removed by the urinary system.

Asbestos is used to make a building material that does not burn. Asbestos was used in the ceilings or walls of older buildings.

Perspiration is a liquid that is made by the body. It contains water, salt, and wastes from your blood.

This firefighter wears a face mask and special clothes for protection from chemicals.

The Urinary System

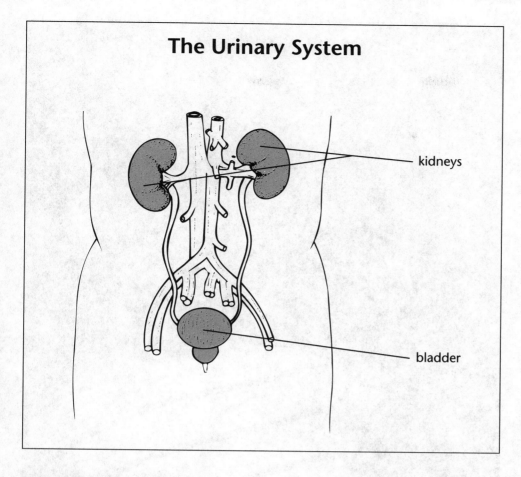

kidneys

bladder

Your kidneys make urine when they remove liquid waste from your blood.

The Urinary System

Your two **kidneys** are the most important part of the urinary system. The kidneys are in the lower back. Their job is to remove liquid waste from the blood. Kidneys make **urine** when they remove waste. Another organ, the **bladder**, holds the urine until you are ready to **urinate**.

This is how the urinary system gets rid of waste.

1. Blood vessels carry blood to the kidneys.
2. Kidneys remove waste from the blood and make urine.
3. Urine leaves each kidney through a tube.
4. Each tube carries urine to the bladder.
5. The bladder holds urine.
6. Urine leaves the body when you urinate.

Problems and Care of the Urinary System

Many people get bladder **infections**. You may have a bladder infection if you notice a painful or

Urine is the liquid waste that is made by the kidneys.

To **urinate** is to rid the body of urine.

Infections are caused by germs growing in all or part of the body.

23

You can help keep your urinary system healthy by drinking six to eight glasses of water each day.

burning feeling when you urinate. You may notice a bad odor or see blood in your urine. You should see your doctor if you think you have an infection.

Kidney stones are another problem for some people. Small stones form in the kidneys and can cause pain. A doctor can treat and remove kidney stones.

You can keep your urinary system healthy by drinking six to eight glasses of water each day. See your doctor if you have a problem when you urinate. See your doctor if you have blood in your urine.

Your body must breathe in oxygen to be healthy. It must also breathe out carbon dioxide. Your urinary system must get rid of the liquid waste made by the body. Caring for your body's systems will help you have a healthy body.

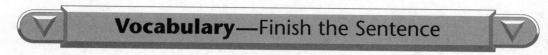

Vocabulary—Finish the Sentence

Choose a word or words in the box to complete each sentence. Write the words on the correct lines.

polluted	asbestos	respiratory system
infection	kidneys	air sacs

1. There are millions of tiny _____ in the lungs.

2. Air that is _____ is dirty and unhealthy.

3. A bladder _____ can make it painful to urinate.

4. Your _____ takes in oxygen and gives off carbon dioxide.

5. Your _____ make urine when they remove liquid waste from the body.

6. A building material called _____ can badly damage your lungs.

Comprehension—Write the Questions

Below are the answers for some questions from this chapter. Read each answer. Then write your own question on the line above each answer. Use the question words to help you. The first one is done for you.

1. What **is the job of the urinary system?**

   The urinary system's job is to clean the blood by removing liquid waste.

2. Where_____

   Oxygen enters the body through the mouth and nose.

3. Who _____

A doctor can treat and remove kidney stones.

4. What _____

You should wear a face mask when working around dangerous gases or asbestos.

5. What _____

The lungs are the most important organs in the respiratory system.

Critical Thinking—Fact or Opinion

A **fact** is a true statement. An **opinion** is a statement that tells what a person thinks.

Fact=Austin is the capital of Texas.

Opinion=Austin is a beautiful city.

Write **Fact** next to each fact below. Write **Opinion** next to each opinion. You should find two sentences that are opinions.

_____ 1. Drinking six to eight glasses of water each day will help keep your urinary system healthy.

_____ 2. Asbestos is harmful to the lungs.

_____ 3. Your respiratory system is the easiest to keep healthy.

_____ 4. Smoking can cause lung disease.

_____ 5. Your heart is the hardest-working organ in your body.

_____ 6. Small kidney stones can cause pain.

_____ 7. You might have a bladder infection if you have a painful feeling when you urinate.

Your Nervous and Endocrine Systems

Think About as You Read

- How does your brain help you think, walk, and breathe?
- Why does your body need hormones?
- How should you care for your body's systems?

All of your body systems must work together for you to be healthy.

The systems of your body perform important jobs. They digest food and get rid of wastes. They take in oxygen and get rid of carbon dioxide. Your body also has two systems that control the way all of the other systems work.

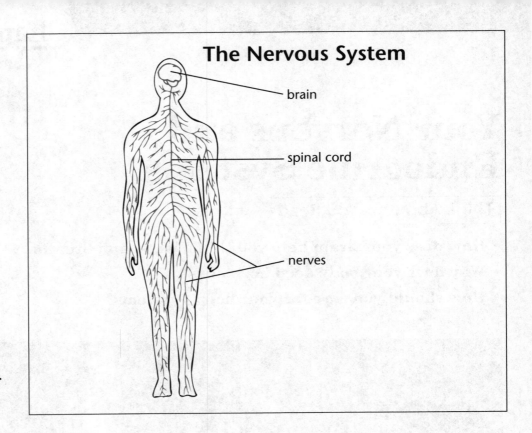

The Nervous System

brain

spinal cord

nerves

Your nervous system controls your thinking, your heart, your breathing, and your movements.

The Nervous System

Your **nervous system** controls everything you do. It controls your thinking and learning. It controls the way your heart pumps and the way you move.

Your nervous system has three parts. The three parts are your brain, your **spinal cord**, and your nerves.

Your nervous system is made of nerve cells. Nerve cells carry messages to different parts of the body. Nerve cells have long **fibers.** The nerves in your body are groups of nerve fibers.

Your **spinal cord** is a thick row of nerves that goes down the center of your back.

Thin, threadlike parts attached to nerve cells are nerve **fibers**

The Brain and Spinal Cord

Your brain is the most important part of the nervous system. It controls the way the nervous system works. The brain is made of nerve cells.

The brain has three parts. Each part of your brain does a different job.

1. The **cerebrum** controls your thinking, talking, and learning. You use your cerebrum when you do math, read, or spell.

2. The **cerebellum** controls the way your body moves. The cerebellum sends messages to your muscles so you can control the way you move. When you ride your bike, you are using your cerebellum.

3. The **medulla** controls your body's systems. It controls your breathing and the beating of your heart. It controls the work of the stomach and the small intestine. It controls the kidneys. Your medulla works even when you are asleep.

Your spinal cord is a thick group of nerves that goes down the center of your back. The spinal cord begins at your brain. It ends below your ribs. The spinal cord is protected by the bones of your spine. The nerves of the spinal cord are connected to nerves in all parts of your body. Nerves in different parts of the body are also connected to the spinal cord.

How does the nervous system work? Your brain sends messages through your nerves to all parts of your body. Nerves in different parts of your body send messages to the brain. These messages allow you to move. The messages also allow you to see, feel, smell, taste, and hear.

Taking Care of Your Nervous System

You should care for your nervous system by protecting your head and spinal cord. Always wear a helmet when you ride your bike or your skateboard.

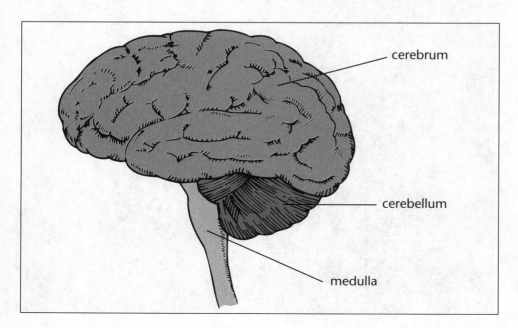

cerebrum

cerebellum

medulla

The most important part of the nervous system is the brain. It has three parts.

Protect your head when you swim. Many people hurt their heads in diving accidents. Never dive into water unless you know it is deep enough for diving.

Protect your head and spinal cord when riding in a car. Always wear a seat belt when riding in a car.

To care for your nervous system, you should get enough sleep. Do not use drugs incorrectly or alcohol. They can destroy the nerve cells of the brain.

Your Endocrine System

Your **endocrine system** has **glands** that make **hormones**. The glands send hormones into the blood. Your blood carries them to different parts of the body. Every hormone does a different job. Your body cannot work and grow properly without these hormones.

How do some of your glands help you? Your **pituitary gland** controls the way all of the other endocrine glands work. It also makes a growth hormone. This hormone controls the growth of your bones.

Your **endocrine system** makes chemicals that help your body work and grow properly.

The **glands** are parts of the body that make chemicals needed by the body.

Hormones are chemicals made by organs in the endocrine system to affect other parts of the body.

Wear a helmet whenever you need to protect your head.

30

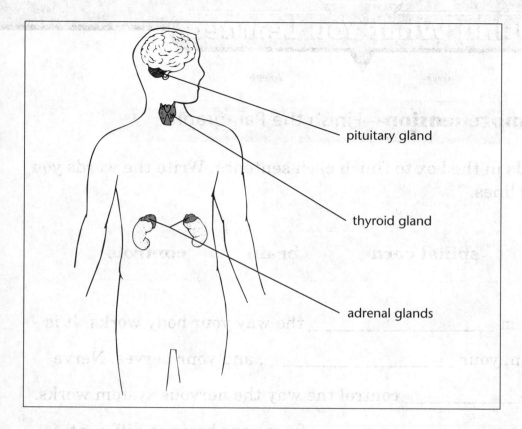

pituitary gland

thyroid gland

adrenal glands

Your endocrine system makes the hormones your body needs. Each hormone does a different job.

Your **adrenal glands** make **adrenaline**. This hormone helps your body deal with **stress**. When a person is very frightened, adrenaline makes the heart beat faster. Adrenaline makes people feel stronger and breathe faster.

Your **thyroid gland** makes a hormone that controls how fast your body uses food. Sometimes the thyroid gland does not make enough of this hormone. Then the body uses food slowly. This causes people to gain weight. The thyroid gland may make too much of this hormone. This can cause people to lose weight. A doctor can treat you if your thyroid gland makes too much or too little of this hormone.

Care for your endocrine system by taking care of your **physical health**. Eat healthy meals and get enough sleep. Try to exercise at least three times a week. Visit your doctor if you think you have a health problem.

You depend on your nervous and endocrine systems for good health. These two systems control the way your other body systems work for you.

Your **adrenal glands** make a hormone that helps the body handle fear and danger.

Stress is the way the body responds to different kinds of demands.

Physical health is how you take care of your body.

31

Comprehension—Finish the Paragraph

Use the word or words in the box to finish each sentence. Write the words you choose on the correct lines.

messages	spinal cord	brain	controls

Your nervous system _____ the way your body works. It is made up of your brain, your _____ , and your nerves. Nerve cells in your _____ control the way the nervous system works. Other nerve cells carry _____ from your brain to different parts of your body.

Vocabulary—Using Vocabulary

Use each word to write a complete sentence about your nervous or endocrine system.

1. nervous system _____

_____

2. endocrine system _____

_____

3. hormones _____

_____

4. spinal cord _____

_____

5. thyroid gland _____

_____

Critical Thinking—Cause and Effect

A **cause** is something that makes something else happen. What happens is called the **effect**.

Cause=It was raining.

Effect=The dog got wet.

Read each pair of sentences below. Decide which one is the cause (what happens first). Decide which one is the effect (what happens next). Write **Cause** or **Effect** next to each sentence. The first one is done for you.

1. **Cause** Your cerebrum controls your thinking, talking, and learning.

   Effect You understand your math homework.

2. _____ You wear a helmet when riding your bike.

   _____ You want to protect your nervous system.

3. _____ Your thyroid does not make enough of the hormone that controls how fast your body uses food.

   _____ You have been gaining a great deal of weight.

4. _____ Your medulla controls your body's systems.

   _____ You do not have to remember to breathe or to make your heart beat.

5. _____ You can swim at the neighborhood swimming pool.

   _____ The cerebellum controls the way your body moves.

6. _____ Nerves send messages to your brain.

   _____ You are able to hear, taste, smell, feel, and see.

UNIT 2

Family Health

Who are the people you really care about? You may care a lot about the members of your family or the family you live with. You may also care about your good friends.

To have good health, you must learn to make good decisions. You may learn these decision-making skills from your family or the family you live with. One day you may teach these skills to your own children.

Have You Ever Wondered ?

▼ Our families meet many of our needs. Which needs?
▼ People see many changes in their bodies during the teen years. What kinds of changes?
▼ People who marry after the age of 22 often have better marriages. Why?

As you read this unit, think about things you can do to get along better with your family or the family you live with and your friends.

34

Living with Your Family

- **What are five different kinds of families?**
- **What kinds of problems do families have?**
- **How can you get along better with your family?**

Family members enjoy doing things together.

Social health is the way you get along with others.

Emotional health is the way you live with your feelings.

You are a member of a family. Your family may share your good times and bad times.

Your family can help you in many ways. Getting along with the family you live with helps your physical health, **social health**, and **emotional health**.

Kinds of Families

Each family is different. Each family has its own rules and problems. Most families can tell stories about their special times together.

Here are five different kinds of families.

1. The **traditional family** has a mother and a father and one or more children.
2. The single-parent family has one parent and one or more children. Sometimes another adult who is not related to the family lives with the family.
3. A stepfamily has one **natural parent**, one stepparent, and one or more children. A stepparent is related to the family by marriage.
4. An **extended family** has one or both parents, one or more children, and other family members living in a home.
5. A **foster family** has adults who take care of one or more children because the children's natural parents cannot care for them.

A **natural parent** is related to the child by blood.

How Does Your Family Meet Your Needs?

Your family can meet your physical needs by giving you food and clothing. Your family also gives you a home in which to live.

In this extended family, the parents, the baby, and other family members live together.

Acceptance is the feeling that others like you and enjoy being with you.

Responsibilities are jobs you do that show you can be trusted to do things well.

Self-esteem is the good feelings you have about yourself.

Your **values** are your ideas about what is important.

Your family can meet your emotional needs by helping you feel love, **acceptance**, and success. You feel acceptance when you are loved even if you make mistakes or have problems. Your family gives you **responsibilities** to allow you to have success. You have high **self-esteem** when you know your family believes in you.

Your family also helps you learn **values**. The values in some families are to work hard, to have good manners, to be kind, and to be honest. Your values help you decide how to act.

Problems in Families

Every family has problems. Sometimes a parent loses a job. Sometimes a member of the family is very sick. Some families do not make enough money to buy the things they need. Drugs and alcohol cause terrible problems in some families.

Sometimes teen-agers have problems in a family. Their parents may not like their friends, their clothes, or their music.

Your family can help you meet your emotional needs for love, acceptance, and success.

Work at getting along with your family. Speak with respect to family members. Be a good listener.

Leslie solved her family problem. She wanted to spend more time with her friends. Leslie told her mother and stepfather how she felt. Then she talked to them about how well she handled her responsibilities at home and at school. Leslie's parents decided to let her spend more time with her friends. They trusted her to make good decisions while she was with her friends.

Building a Strong Family

Talk to your family. Tell your family about the things that make you happy, sad, and angry. Speak with respect to family members. Be a good listener.

You can do five things to get along better with your family.

1. Do your share of jobs and chores at home.
2. Listen when family members talk about their problems and their successes.
3. Show respect for others.
4. Do things that you enjoy with your family.
5. Celebrate special holidays and birthdays with your family.

Learn to get along with your family. Then you will have the skills to get along with others when you are away from home.

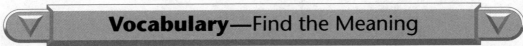

Vocabulary—Find the Meaning

On the line write the word or words that best complete each sentence.

1. The way you get along with others is your _____ .
   social health   **extended family**   **emotional health**

2. A mother, a father, and one or more children make up the

   _____ .
   good decisions   **traditional family**   **single-parent family**

3. The jobs you do that show you can be trusted to do things well are your

   _____ .
   responsibilities   **values**   **problems**

4. A _____ is the mother or father who is related to a
   child by blood.
   foster family   **stepparent**   **natural parent**

5. Your ideas about what is important are your _____ .
   friends   **chores**   **values**

Comprehension—Write the Questions

Below are the answers for some questions from this chapter. Read each
answer. Then write your own question on the line above each answer. Use the
question words to help you. The first one is done for you.

1. What **is a single-parent family?** _____
   A single-parent family has one parent and one or more children.

2. Who _____
   Your family helps you learn values.

3. Why _____

Your family gives you responsibilities to allow you to have success.

4. What_____

Your family meets your physical needs for food and clothing.

5. How _____

A stepparent is related to a family by marriage.

6. What_____

The values in some families are to work hard and to be honest.

Critical Thinking—Analogies

Use a word or words in the box to finish each sentence.

talking	emotional need	self-esteem
stepfamily	values	

1. Good manners are to _____ as chores are to responsibilities.

2. Physical need is to food as _____ is to acceptance.

3. Responsibilities are to jobs as _____ is to good feelings.

4. Sharing ideas is to _____ as listening is to understanding others.

5. Single-parent family is to one parent as _____ is to one natural parent and one stepparent.

Building Relationships

Think About as You Read

- **Which communication skills can help you get along with others?**
- **How can you build strong friendships?**
- **Why should teen-agers say no to intimate sexual behavior?**

Boys and girls may start to form friendships with each other during the teen years.

Relationships are the way you get along with others.

Adam felt nervous at his first school dance. He had never danced with a girl. Building new **relationships** can be difficult. In this chapter you will read about ways to build relationships.

Improving Communication Skills

Share your ideas with others. This will help you build good relationships. These four **communication** skills can help you get along with others.

1. Be a good listener. Listen to what other people say. Then share your own ideas.
2. Do not talk about other people. People often find out what others say about them. People may be angry with you for talking about them.
3. Think carefully before you speak. Do not say things you may later feel sorry about. You may say the wrong things when you are angry or unhappy.
4. Use "I" messages when you talk about your feelings. Talk about how you think and feel instead of blaming others.

Different Kinds of Relationships

Every person needs love and friendship to have good emotional and social health. To have loving relationships, you must show people that you care.

Your first loving relationships are with your family. As you grow, you form other friendships. Every person needs friends.

Communication is sharing your thoughts or feelings with others.

Learn how to share your ideas and feelings with others.

Choose your friends carefully. Show your friends that you care about them.

How can you build strong friendships? First, you must like yourself and accept yourself. Then others will like you, too. Choose your friends carefully. It is important that you share the same values and enjoy some of the same activities.

To be a good friend, try to understand the feelings of others. Show your friends that you respect and trust them. Be kind to your friends.

During the teen years, groups of boys and girls spend time together. They may go as a group to the movies or to a park. Some teens start to date.

Dating

Dating becomes important to some people during the early teen years. Other teens do not feel ready to date until they are older. Many parents make rules about the age when teens can start dating.

Some teens have low self-esteem if they do not have many dates. There are other ways teens can build self-esteem. Sharing activities and interests with friends builds self-esteem. Learning new skills also builds self-esteem.

How should you choose a person to date? You date a person you find attractive. The person should share your values. Your date should enjoy some of your interests. Your date should also have respect for you and your decisions.

You should show responsible behavior when you are on a date. Show good manners. Do not use alcohol or other drugs. Return home at the time your parents ask you to be home.

Sexual Behavior

All people have **sexual** feelings. Your sexual behavior is the way you show your sexual feelings.

Sexual behavior can be smiling at people of the **opposite sex** to show you like them. For some people sexual behavior can be holding hands, hugging, and kissing. Married adults have intimate sexual behavior.

Sexual describes anything that has to do with being a male or a female.

The **opposite sex** is the one that is different from your own. If you are a male, a member of the opposite sex is a female.

Holding hands is one kind of sexual behavior. You should avoid high-risk sexual behavior.

AIDS is a disease in which the body cannot fight germs. AIDS can be spread through body liquids. There is no cure for AIDS.

Sexually transmitted diseases are diseases that can be spread from person to person through intimate sexual behavior.

Pregnancy is having one or more unborn children growing inside a female's body.

Abstinence is choosing not to do something. People may choose not to have intimate sexual behavior.

Risk behaviors are behaviors that can harm your health.

Wellness means having good physical, social, and emotional health. Wellness is the highest health goal.

You may feel pressure to have intimate sexual behavior when dating. As a teen-ager you are making a wise decision when you say no to intimate sexual behavior. Here are three reasons for a teen-ager to say no.

1. You can get **AIDS** and other **sexually transmitted diseases** through intimate sexual behavior. AIDS is a terrible disease that kills people.

2. Intimate sexual behavior can lead to **pregnancy**.

3. Intimate sexual behavior can cause stress. You can feel guilty. You may worry about pregnancy. You may also worry about getting AIDS and other diseases. Your date may want you to have intimate sexual behavior again. Other people may learn about your intimate sexual behavior from your date.

Decide before a date what type of sexual behavior is right for you. It is healthy and safe to choose **abstinence**. Try hard to avoid **risk behaviors**.

The chart below shows three problems you may worry about when you say no to intimate sexual behavior. The chart also gives you answers for these problems. Never let your date talk you into doing something that you do not want to do.

Every person needs love and friendship. Your relationships can help you reach your goal of **wellness**.

Dating and Sexual Behavior

Problem:	*Answer:*
1. My date may not want to see me again if I choose abstinence.	1. Your date should enjoy your company without intimate sexual behavior.
2. My friends will laugh at me if they learn I choose abstinence.	2. A real friend never wants you to hurt yourself with a risk behavior.
3. No one will want to date me if I choose abstinence.	3. Other people also choose abstinence. They will want to date you. They will approve of your decision.

Vocabulary—Matching

Match the vocabulary word in **Group B** with its definition from **Group A**. Write the letter of the correct answer on the line.

Group A

_____ 1. This means you choose not to do something.

_____ 2. This is a disease in which the body cannot fight germs.

_____ 3. These can harm your health.

_____ 4. You use good communication skills to build these.

Group B

a. AIDS

b. relationships

c. abstinence

d. risk behaviors

Comprehension—True or False

Write **True** next to each sentence that is true. Write **False** next to each sentence that is false. There are two false sentences.

_____ 1. Being a good listener can help you get along with others.

_____ 2. Only adults have sexual feelings.

_____ 3. AIDS is spread through intimate sexual behavior.

_____ 4. Sharing activities and interests with friends lowers self-esteem.

On the lines that follow, rewrite the two false sentences to make them true.

_____

_____

_____

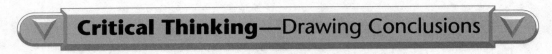

Read the paragraph. Then use the six steps to decide what to do about building new relationships. Write a complete sentence to answer each question.

Imagine that there is a new student, who is of the opposite sex, in your class. You enjoy doing healthy activities after school with this new student. But your other friends are angry because you don't spend as much time with them.

Step 1. What is the problem?

_____

Step 2. What are two ways to solve the problem?

_____

_____

Step 3. What is one consequence, or possible result, for each choice listed in Step 2?

_____

_____

Step 4. Which choice do you think is best?

_____

Step 5. What can you do to put your decision into action?

_____

_____

Step 6. Think about your decision. Why was this the best choice for you?

_____

_____

Growth During the Teen Years

Think About as You Read

- **How do males change during puberty?**
- **How do females change during puberty?**
- **What emotional and social changes take place during the teen years?**

During the teen years, your body changes. You will have social and emotional changes, too.

Fourteen-year-old Pablo has more hair on his face than he did last year. His body has changed in other ways since he was 13. He has grown taller. He has gained weight. He has more hair on his body. Pablo is going through the changes of **puberty**. In this chapter you will learn how males and females change during puberty.

Puberty is the time when the sex organs and the sex glands begin to work.

49

Understanding Puberty

Reproductive organs are the parts of the body that allow males and females to produce children.

Mature describes something or someone that is fully grown or fully developed.

Every person is born with **reproductive organs**. In order for a male and a female to have a baby, their reproductive organs must **mature**. The reproductive organs slowly mature during puberty.

Many changes take place in your body at puberty. You grow taller. You gain weight faster. More hair grows on your body. Oil glands and sweat glands work much harder. Your skin and hair may be more oily. You may have pimples and blackheads. You may need to wash your hair more often.

Puberty is different for each person. Puberty affects males and females differently.

Some people go through puberty in the early teen years. For others puberty starts later. Some people grow and develop much faster than others. For others puberty lasts longer. By the end of puberty, every person's body has matured into the body of an adult.

Puberty is different for each person. By the end of puberty, every person has a mature body.

Hormones cause the changes of puberty. Males and females have different sex hormones.

Hormones cause all of the changes during puberty. You have learned that the endocrine glands make hormones. The pituitary gland sends hormones into the blood during puberty. These hormones make your bones grow. They make your sex glands start to work. Then the sex glands make their own hormones.

Males and Puberty

During puberty a male's **testes** start to produce male sex hormones. These hormones cause hair to grow on a male's face and chest. They cause a male's voice to become deeper. The male sex hormones cause his shoulders to become wider.

Male hormones make the male sex organs mature. The testes start to produce **sperm cells**. When a sperm cell from a male enters an egg cell inside a female, she becomes pregnant.

The **testes** are the male endocrine glands that make male sex hormones.

Sperm cells are male reproductive cells.

During puberty the ovaries start to make female hormones.

Ovaries are female sex glands that produce female hormones and egg cells.

Menstruation is the three-to-seven-day period when the egg cell flows out of the uterus with some blood.

The **uterus** is the female organ where a developing baby grows during pregnancy.

Females and Puberty

A female has two **ovaries**. The ovaries have thousands of tiny egg cells. During puberty the ovaries start to make female hormones. These hormones make a female's breasts grow larger. Her hips grow wider. The egg cells in the ovaries mature.

Menstruation also begins during puberty. Most females begin menstruation at about age 12. About every 28 days, an egg cell leaves one of the ovaries. It travels through one of the two **Fallopian tubes** to the **uterus**. Menstruation starts about two weeks after an egg cell leaves the ovary. Menstruation starts if a female is not pregnant. During menstruation the egg cell flows out of the uterus with some blood. This flow is also called a "period." The flow of blood lasts between three and seven days.

A female may have a period about every 28 days. Some females may have a period every 25 days or every 35 days. Sometimes it takes a few years for a female's period to become regular. Then she will usually have her period around the same time each month.

Many females have questions about their periods. They should ask their parents, doctor, or school nurse any questions they have.

Emotional and Social Changes During Puberty

Many teen-agers have low self-esteem during puberty. They may feel unhappy with their changing bodies. Some teen-agers mature earlier than their friends. These teens may think they look too grown-up. Other teen-agers mature later than their friends. These teens may have low self-esteem because they look less grown-up than their friends.

Teen-agers want more freedom and responsibility as they grow older. They may want to hold a job and drive a car. Teens often want more freedom from their parents. They want to spend more time with friends and less time with their family. Many teens no longer like the same music, dances, or clothes that their parents enjoy. Spending time alone can be important to teen-agers.

Many teens start dating. They must think about having responsible sexual behavior. They must avoid risk behaviors when dating.

Every person must go through the changes of puberty. By making responsible decisions, teens can reach the goal of wellness.

Many teen-agers want to spend more time with their friends and less time with their parents.

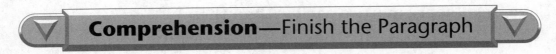

Comprehension—Finish the Paragraph

Use the words in the box to finish each sentence. Write the words you choose on the correct lines.

glands	hair	taller	different
organs	deeper	hormones	wider

During the teen years you and your friends grow and develop at

_____ rates. All of the changes of puberty are caused by

_____ . Hormones help you to grow _____ .

They make more _____ grow on your body. Hormones make

your oil and sweat _____ work harder. They also cause your

reproductive _____ to mature. Male hormones make a male's

voice _____ . Female hormones make a female's hips grow

_____ .

Vocabulary—Using Vocabulary

Use each word to write a complete sentence about growth during the teen years.

1. puberty_____

_____

2. mature _____

_____

3. menstruation _____

_____

4. ovaries _____

_____

▽ Critical Thinking—Fact or Opinion ▽

Read each sentence below. Write **Fact** next to each sentence that tells a fact. Write **Opinion** next to each sentence that tells an opinion. You should find four sentences that are opinions.

_____ 1. It is easier for boys to go through puberty than it is for girls.

_____ 2. Every person is born with reproductive organs.

_____ 3. The male's testes produce sperm cells.

_____ 4. Oil and sweat glands work harder during puberty.

_____ 5. It is best to start going through puberty before the age of 13.

_____ 6. Reproductive organs mature during puberty.

_____ 7. Menstruation takes place only if the female is not pregnant.

_____ 8. Every person goes through many changes during puberty.

_____ 9. Making responsible decisions is always easy.

_____10. You should never spend time alone during puberty.

_____11. Many teen-agers want to spend more time with their friends than with their family.

_____12. By the end of puberty, a person's body has matured into that of an adult.

The Life Cycle

Think About as You Read

- How should a female care for her unborn baby?
- What are the five stages of the life cycle?
- What makes each person different from every other person?

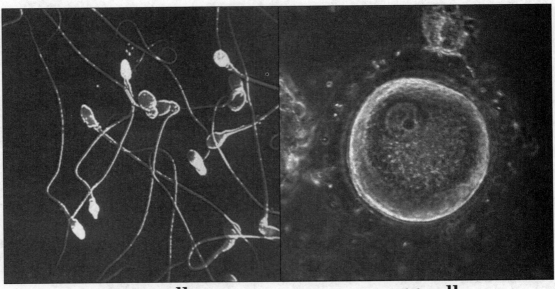

A new life begins when a sperm cell from a male joins an egg cell from the female.

sperm cells   egg cell

The **life cycle** is the five stages of life from birth until death.

Every person begins life as one cell that grows into a baby. People go through different stages of the **life cycle**. At the end of the life cycle, all living things die.

A New Life Begins

A new life begins when a sperm cell from a male joins an egg cell from a female. The two cells join in one of the female's Fallopian tubes. When the sperm cell and the egg cell join, they form a **fertilized egg**. The female becomes pregnant. This fertilized egg can grow into a baby.

The fertilized egg travels from the Fallopian tube into the uterus. Inside the uterus it grows into a baby. First, the fertilized egg divides into two cells. Then these cells divide again and again. Soon there are millions of cells. The cells begin to form organs. By the end of one month, the baby has a tiny beating heart.

The growing baby gets its nutrients and oxygen through an **umbilical cord**. This cord attaches the mother's uterus and the baby's navel. Nutrients and oxygen from the mother's body go through the blood vessels in the umbilical cord to the baby.

A pregnancy should last about nine months. At the end of that time, the baby is ready to be born.

The birth of a baby begins with **labor**. During labor the muscles of the female's uterus push the baby down towards the **vagina**. At birth the baby comes out of the mother's vagina. The head should come out first. The umbilical cord is cut right after birth.

The **umbilical cord** is a thick cord made of blood vessels that connects the baby's navel to its mother's uterus.

Labor is the physical work done by a female's body to give birth to a baby.

The **vagina** is the part of a female's body that goes from the uterus to outside the body.

Nine Months of Pregnancy

third month

sixth month

ninth month

A baby should grow in its mother's uterus for nine months.

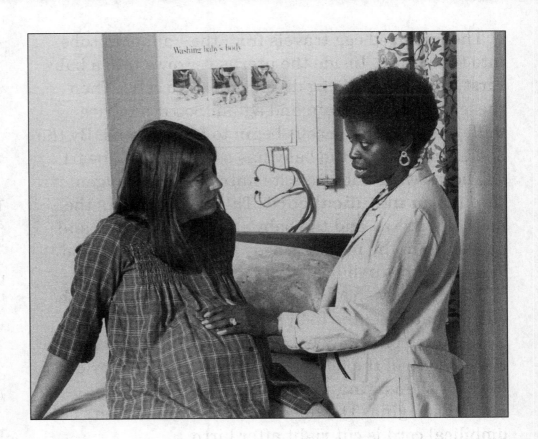

There are many things a pregnant female should do to have a healthy baby.

Sometimes the baby cannot be born by passing through the vagina. Doing so may be dangerous for the mother or for the baby. If there is a problem, the female may have an operation called a **Cesarean section** to have the baby.

Caring for the Unborn Baby

To have a healthy baby, a pregnant female should take care of herself in these six ways.

1. See a doctor as often as necessary for checkups.
2. Eat a healthy diet. A pregnant female must get enough nutrients. She needs extra calcium and iron in her diet.
3. Get enough sleep and rest.
4. Never use drugs in ways that are not correct. Do not drink alcohol. Drugs and alcohol can damage the new baby's brain and body.
5. Do not smoke. The babies of smoking mothers are often smaller and less healthy.
6. Do not take any medicine without checking with a doctor.

The Life Cycle

There are five stages in the human life cycle.

1. The nine months of pregnancy are the first stage of the life cycle.

2. Childhood is the time from birth to the teen years. The new baby grows. It learns to sit, walk, and talk. During this stage the child is always learning new skills.

3. During the teen years, the teen-ager grows into an adult. By the age of 19, many teens have reached their full height. They develop new skills. Friendships are especially important.

4. The adult years are from age 20 to about age 65. To have a strong, healthy body, an adult must exercise and have healthy eating habits. Adults may get married and have children. Emotional and social growth continues during the adult years.

5. Older adults are age 65 or older. Many older adults continue to play sports and exercise. They may retire from their jobs. Then they may spend more time doing hobbies. Older adults may develop health problems. This stage of the life cycle ends when the person dies.

Childhood, adult years, and older adult years are three stages of the life cycle.

You inherit many traits from both parents. Some traits are for skin, hair, and eye color.

Each Person Is Different

As you go through the life cycle, many things about you change. The way you look, think, act, or feel may change. Let's look at what makes you special.

You are different from every other person. You were born with your own group of **traits**. Some of your traits have to do with how you look. These traits include your hair color, your skin color, your eye color, and your height. Other traits have to do with the way you act, think, and feel.

You **inherited** many traits from your parents. The egg cell from your mother and the sperm cell from your father each carried information about traits. You know that the sperm and egg joined to form a fertilized egg. This fertilized egg carried traits from both parents.

The kind of person you are begins with inherited traits. But the kind of person you become depends on what happens to you in your **environment**. Your home, family, friends, and your school are part of your environment. Your environment can affect what you learn. It may also affect the skills you have.

Traits are characteristics, such as skin and eye color, that belong to each person.

Inherited means a person received certain traits from his or her parents.

The **environment** includes the people, places, and objects that are around a person.

60

Your family environment makes you different from someone else. Maybe you are the oldest child in the family. You may have the responsibility of taking care of your younger brothers and sisters. If you are the youngest child in a family, you may not have this kind of responsibility. If you have lived in different cities, you may have had different experiences than people who have lived in the same city or town all their lives.

Your environment affects your traits. Try to use your environment to improve your traits. You may have a trait for curly or straight hair. You can learn to take care of your hair so it is clean and healthy.

People are born with many good traits. Use your traits to have success and good health. To do this you should make wise decisions during every stage of the life cycle. Try to make decisions that will help you reach the goal of wellness.

You may have traits that allow you to be good at sports. Work at improving your traits.

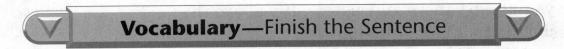

Vocabulary—Finish the Sentence

Choose a word or words in the box to complete each sentence. Write the words on the correct lines.

| life cycle | umbilical cord | inherit | labor | environment |

1. A baby's navel is attached to the mother's uterus by an

   _____ .

2. The characteristics you _____ from your parents are called traits.

3. The people, places, and objects around you are your _____ .

4. The human _____ has five stages.

5. The birth of a baby begins with _____ .

Comprehension—Writing About Health

Answer the following question in complete sentences.

What are three things a pregnant female can do for her unborn baby?

_____

_____

_____

_____

_____

Read each pair of sentences. Write **Cause** next to the sentence that tells a cause. Write **Effect** next to the sentence that tells an effect.

1. _____ A pregnant female takes good care of herself.

    _____ A pregnant female wants to have a healthy baby.

2. _____ You have dark hair and blue eyes.

    _____ You inherited traits from your parents.

3. _____ The person is at the end of his or her life cycle.

    _____ The person dies.

4. _____ The sperm cell from the male joins an egg cell from the female.

    _____ The female becomes pregnant.

5. _____ The muscles of the uterus push down on the baby.

    _____ The baby is born.

6. _____ The baby is able to get its nutrients and oxygen through the umbilical cord.

    _____ The umbilical cord connects the baby's navel to the mother's uterus.

7. _____ You are the oldest child in your family.

    _____ Your parents depend on you to do certain chores.

8. _____ You have success and good health.

    _____ You make wise decisions throughout your life.

Marriage and Parenthood

Think About as You Read

- **What are the right and wrong reasons to get married?**
- **Why are teen-agers too young to be parents?**
- **How should parents care for their children?**

People who get married for the right reasons can be happy together.

Jennifer has been dating Rick for two years. Rick is 17. Jennifer is 16. Jennifer does not get along with her parents. She wants to drop out of school, get a job, and marry Rick. Rick says he is not ready to get married. What do you think Jennifer and Rick should do? In this chapter you will learn how couples can build good marriages and happy families.

People who marry should love and care for each other. They should share important values.

Why Do People Get Married?

There are three very good reasons for a couple to get married. First, the couple shares interests and values. They enjoy being together. Second, they love and care for each other. Third, the couple communicates with each other. They share their feelings and solve problems.

Let's look at four of the wrong reasons people get married.

1. A couple gets married because of family **pressure**. Their parents want them to get married.
2. People get married because of **peer pressure**. Most of their friends are getting married.
3. A couple gets married because the female becomes pregnant.
4. Some people get married because they have an unhappy home life. They are unhappy living with their parents, brothers, and sisters. These people get married to escape family problems.

Pressure is a strong demand.

Peer pressure is the control over your decisions that people of your age try to have.

65

Teen-age mothers have problems. It is hard for them to finish high school and get good jobs.

Teen-age Marriages

Many teens marry because of peer pressure or to escape an unhappy home life. Many teen couples marry because the female is pregnant. Teen-agers often are not ready for family responsibilities.

Most teen marriages are unhappy. Married teen-agers often drop out of high school. Because they have not completed their education, they cannot get good jobs. They cannot earn enough money to buy the things they want or need. Most married teens do not understand the problems and feelings of the other person. They do not enjoy taking care of a home, washing clothes, and cooking meals every day. They want more time to have fun.

Many babies are born to teen-age females who are not married. Teen-age mothers and their babies have many problems. It is hard for teen-age mothers to finish high school and get good jobs. Taking care of their babies keeps teens so busy they have little time for fun. Some teen mothers may become **child abusers.** These teen mothers hurt their children because they are unhappy caring for the children.

Teen-age females should avoid becoming pregnant. They should say no to intimate sexual behavior. They should choose abstinence.

Child abusers are people who hurt children in ways that are not accidents.

66

Happy and Unhappy Marriages

To have a happy marriage, a couple should be mature. Most people who get married after the age of 22 have a better chance at having a happy marriage. People have better marriages when they share goals. Their goals may be to buy a house or have children. Couples must want to share good times and bad times together. They must trust each other. Earning enough money to pay for the things a couple wants and needs also helps a marriage.

Communication helps a marriage. People must share ideas and feelings. Couples should solve problems together. The husband and wife must learn to **compromise**.

To **compromise** means to reach an agreement by having each side give up part of its demands.

Many marriages are not happy. Each year more than one million marriages end in divorce. Couples divorce for many different reasons. Divorce may be the last step for couples who have tried to work things out and to improve their marriage.

Happy couples share ideas and solve problems. They learn how to compromise.

A couple must go to court to get a divorce. A judge must decide whether to allow the couple to divorce. The judge also decides how the divorced couple will divide money and property from their marriage. The judge decides the best way to take care of any children the couple may have.

Most divorced people get married again. They often marry people who have children from another marriage. New stepfamilies are formed.

Counseling can help divorced families. It helps them talk about their feelings. Counseling helps them live with their new families and stepfamilies.

Becoming Parents

Many married couples want to have children. Couples should plan when to have children. They should talk about how many children they want.

Counseling is giving advice and sharing ideas in order to help people solve their problems.

Many married couples want to have children.

68

Parents can help their children have good emotional, physical, and social health.

Children need love, food, and clothes. They need a good home and medical care. They need time and attention from their parents. Parents must be able to take care of their children's needs. Parents need enough money to pay for things their children need.

Many children live in homes with only one parent. The single parent must do the work of both the mother and father. It is a hard job. But many single parents do a fine job.

Parents want their children to have good physical, social, and emotional health. Here are six things parents can do to help their children have wellness.

1. Parents can help their children set goals that can be reached.
2. They can show their children they love them.
3. Parents can teach values to their children.
4. They can teach their children correct behavior.
5. Parents can share ideas and feelings with their children.
6. They can teach their children decision-making skills.

Married people must work hard to have a good marriage and a happy family. Family life helps people have good physical, social, and emotional health.

69

Using What You Learned

Vocabulary—Matching

Match the vocabulary word in **Group B** with its definition from **Group A**.
Write the letter of the correct answer on the line.

Group A

_____ 1. This is the control people your age try to have over your decisions.

_____ 2. A person who hurts a child in a way that is not an accident is called this.

_____ 3. People may need this in order to solve their problems.

_____ 4. Two people give up some of their demands to reach this agreement.

_____ 5. This is a strong demand.

Group B

a. pressure

b. compromise

c. child abuser

d. peer pressure

e. counseling

Comprehension—Write the Answer

Write an answer in a complete sentence to each question.

1. How does peer pressure make people want to get married?

_____

2. Why does communication help a marriage?

_____

3. Who decides the best way to take care of the children of a couple who gets divorced?

_____

4. What kinds of problems do married teen-agers have?

_____

5. How can teen-age females avoid getting pregnant?

_____

6. Why do some divorced families go to counseling?

_____

Critical Thinking—Categories

Read the words in each group. Decide how they are alike. Find the best title in the box for each group. Write the title on the line beside each group.

wrong reasons to marry **divorce**	**parents' responsibilities** **good reasons to marry**

1. share interests and values _____
   love and care for each other
   communicate well

2. marriage problems _____
   end an unhappy marriage
   money and property divided

3. unhappy home life_____
   female gets pregnant
   peer pressure

4. show their children love_____
   teach their children values
   take care of their children's needs

UNIT 3

Drug Abuse

Young people across the nation are doing important work. They have formed groups to teach each other to say no to drugs.

Would you want to hurt your family, lose good friends, and destroy your health? Of course you wouldn't. But millions of drug abusers hurt themselves and others each year. You can protect yourself by learning about drugs. Learn how drugs harm your physical, emotional, and social health. Then learn to say no to peer pressure and to avoid risk behaviors.

Have You Ever Wondered ?

▼ It is dangerous to try drugs or drink alcohol even once. Why?

▼ There is one illegal drug that is abused more often than any other. Which drug?

▼ One drug kills more people than any other. Which one?

▼ Cigarettes can harm people who never smoke. How?

As you read this unit, think of ways to protect your health by saying no to drugs.

JUST SAY NO TO DRUGS

Understanding Drug Abuse

Think About as You Read

- **What are the safe ways to take medicine?**
- **What are three types of drug abuse?**
- **Why do people abuse drugs?**

Kristi Yamaguchi never abused drugs. She wanted to reach her goal of winning a gold medal.

Skater Kristi Yamaguchi reached her goal in 1992. She won the gold medal for the United States at the Winter Olympics. Kristi had practiced many hours each day to become a skating star. One of the reasons she was able to reach her goal was that she never abused drugs. Kristi believes you must say no to drugs if you want to reach your goals.

Some drugs are medicines that can be bought only with a prescription from a doctor.

What Are Drugs?

There are many kinds of drugs. A drug is a chemical or other substance that changes the way your body works. A drug can also affect your mind, feelings, and actions. Most drugs cure, try to cure, or prevent diseases.

Some drugs are medicines, such as **antibiotics**. You may need a prescription to buy some medicines. You can buy other medicines, such as aspirin, without a prescription.

There are also dangerous drugs. Many of these drugs are illegal. It is against the law to buy, sell, make, or use illegal drugs. **Heroin** is an illegal drug.

Using Medicine Safely

There are two groups of medicines. There are prescription drugs and over-the-counter drugs.

Antibiotics are medicines that can kill germs that cause disease.

Heroin is a dangerous, habit-forming drug.

75

You can buy prescription drugs only with a prescription from a doctor. Antibiotics are one kind of prescription drug. Read and follow the directions on the label. Be sure to take the drug. Tell your doctor if you have **side effects** from taking the drug. Do not share your medicine with others. You should never take another person's prescription drug. The drug may be dangerous for you.

Always follow your doctor's directions when taking prescribed medicine. If you are sick, your doctor may tell you to take an antibiotic for ten days. You may not get well if you take it for less than ten days.

You do not need a prescription to buy an over-the-counter drug. If you are taking a prescription drug, check with your doctor before using an over-the-counter drug. Use over-the-counter drugs correctly. Read labels on over-the-counter drugs. Follow the directions. Pay attention to warnings and possible side effects. Do not use medicine after the **expiration date** on the label has passed. Never use medicine if the seal is broken when you buy it. Never drink alcohol when you take medicine.

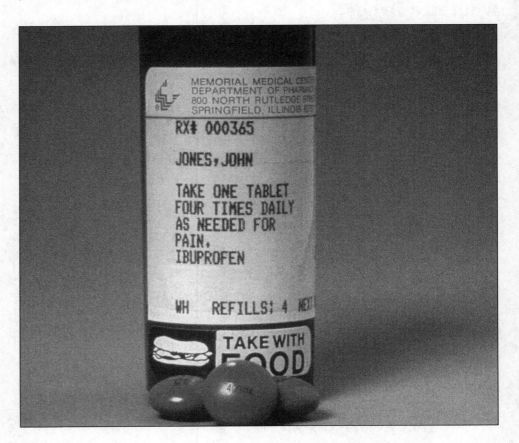

76

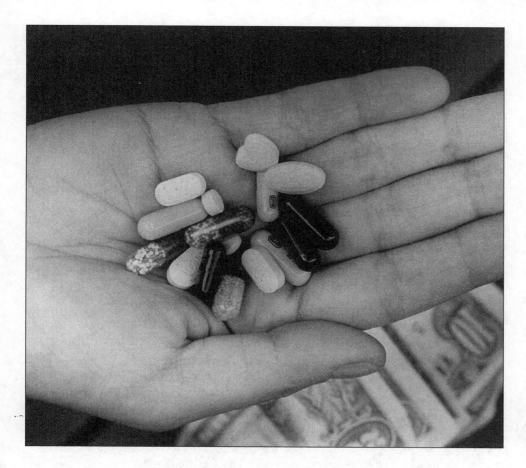

Drug abuse is using drugs in a way that is not correct. Many kinds of drugs are abused.

What Is Drug Abuse?

Drug abuse is using a drug in a way that is not correct. Drug abuse is also using a drug for no medical reason. There are three kinds of drug abuse. The first is when people do not take over-the-counter or prescription drugs correctly. Perhaps a person should take one pill three times a day. Instead the person takes all three pills at once. The second kind of drug abuse is the use of any illegal drug. The third type of drug abuse is when people take prescription drugs that belong to someone else.

How Does Abusing Drugs Harm People?

People who abuse drugs can develop a strong **dependence** on them. People with physical dependence must have drugs for their bodies to feel normal. People with emotional dependence must use drugs to avoid having certain unpleasant feelings. Dependence makes it very hard to stop using drugs.

Dependence is the very strong need for drugs.

77

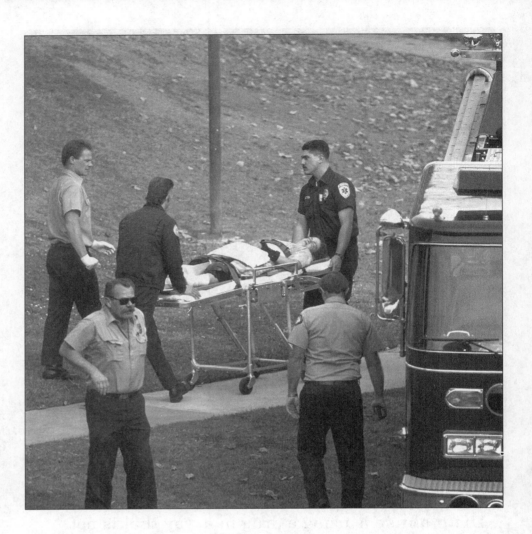

Some people take large amounts of a drug. This can be very dangerous.

Tolerance means the body needs more of a drug to get the same feeling it once felt with smaller amounts.

To feel **high** means to have a good feeling that lasts a short time. People sometimes get high from abusing drugs.

People who abuse drugs develop **tolerance**. People may feel **high** from taking a small amount of a drug. Later they need to take more of the drug to feel good. Taking large amounts of a drug can be dangerous. It can cause death.

Many people use needles to get drugs such as heroin into their bodies. They often share their needles with other drug abusers. Sharing needles can spread AIDS. Sharing needles can also spread other dangerous diseases that may cause death.

You break the law when you buy, sell, make, or use illegal drugs. You may go to jail.

Illegal drugs are very expensive. A drug abuser can spend hundreds of dollars a day to buy drugs. Most drug abusers do not have the money they need to buy their drugs. They may kill and steal to get money. Some drug abusers sell drugs to get money.

Why Do People Abuse Drugs?

Here are five reasons people abuse drugs.

1. People abuse drugs because of peer pressure. They decide to abuse drugs because others are doing it.
2. People abuse drugs to deal with stress. They abuse drugs to forget their problems.
3. People may abuse drugs because they want to know how the drug will make them feel.
4. Some people do not have friends. They think abusing drugs will help them make friends with other drug abusers.
5. People abuse drugs to show they do not have to listen to their parents or other people who make rules.

Who Abuses Drugs?

Most drug abusers are unhappy people without goals. They have low self-esteem. Their own friends may abuse drugs.

You can often tell when people are abusing drugs. Their behavior may suddenly change. Getting and abusing drugs is their main goal in life. They may no longer care about their family and friends. They may stop caring about their appearance.

Drug abusers don't care about many things. Their main goal is to get and abuse drugs.

Drug abusers may stop caring about their schoolwork. They may skip classes. Their grades may be lower. Many drug abusers drop out of school.

Drug abusers say they can stop using drugs at any time. But a drug habit is hard to break. Drug abusers usually need help to get off and stay off drugs.

How to Feel Good Without Drugs

People with good emotional health do not need to abuse drugs to feel good. They do enjoyable activities to feel good. Listening to music or working on a hobby are ways to feel good. Other people like running, swimming, and riding a bike. Some people join clubs. Many people enjoy spending time with close friends who do not abuse drugs.

All people have stress in their lives. Using drugs is a dangerous way to handle stress. Exercising and getting enough rest are better ways. Talking about your problems with a trusted adult is a healthy way to handle stress.

Find ways to feel good without abusing drugs. Always remember that drugs can ruin your life.

People can feel good without using drugs. Exercising is one good way to handle stress.

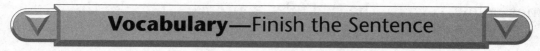

Using What You Learned

Vocabulary—Finish the Sentence

Choose a word or words in the box to complete each sentence. Write the words on the correct lines.

drug abuse	high
dependence	side effects

1. Tell your doctor if you have any _____ from a prescription medicine.

2. Using a drug in a way that is not correct is _____ .

3. People who must have drugs to feel normal have a physical and emotional _____ on the drugs.

4. Sometimes people abuse drugs to feel _____ .

Comprehension—True or False

Write **True** next to each sentence that is true. Write **False** next to each sentence that is false. There are two false sentences.

_____ 1. A drug is a chemical or other substance that changes the way your body works.

_____ 2. Illegal drugs do not cost very much.

_____ 3. Drug abusers who build up a tolerance need less of the drug to feel good.

_____ 4. You should read the labels on all medicines.

_____ 5. Sharing needles can spread AIDS.

On the lines below, rewrite the two false sentences to make them true.

_____

_____

_____

Critical Thinking—Drawing Conclusions

Read the paragraph. Then use the six steps to decide what to do about drug abuse. Write a complete sentence to answer each question.

Imagine that your best friend is thinking about trying some illegal drugs. Your friend wants you to try them, too. On your way home from a movie, your friend shows you the illegal drugs.

Step 1. What is the problem?

_____

Step 2. What are two ways to solve the problem?

_____

Step 3. What is one consequence, or result, for each choice listed in Step 2?

_____

Step 4. Which choice do you think is best?

_____

Step 5. What can you do to put your decision into action?

_____

Step 6. Think about your decision. Why was this the best choice for you?

_____

The Abuse of Drugs

Think About as You Read

- What are the dangers of marijuana, heroin, and cocaine?
- How can you say no to abusing drugs?
- Where can drug addicts get help?

An important goal is to finish school. Reach your goals by always saying no to drugs.

Ramón's goal is to finish high school. It is not an easy goal. He knows he cannot reach his goal if he abuses drugs. Ramón always says no when someone asks him to abuse drugs.

Which Drugs Are Abused?

Codeine is a
prescription drug that
reduces pain.

Codeine and **tranquilizers** are prescription drugs. Some people abuse these drugs. They take much larger **doses** than their doctors order.

Tranquilizers are
prescription drugs that
have a calming effect
because they slow down
the nervous system.

People use **marijuana** more than any other illegal drug. People often smoke it to feel high. But marijuana does not always give people a good feeling.

Doses are amounts of
medicine that a person
takes at one time.

Marijuana can make people forget things. People who use marijuana may care less about reaching their goals. The drug makes people think and act more slowly. People who are using the drug find it hard to ride a bike or drive a car. Marijuana smoke can cause lung **cancer**.

Cancer is a disease in
which unhealthy cells
multiply too rapidly and
destroy body parts.

Marijuana can cause emotional dependence. People believe they must use marijuana to feel good. Some experts believe that marijuana is often the first drug people abuse.

A **narcotic** is a drug
that reduces pain and
causes dependence.

Heroin is a very dangerous drug. It is a **narcotic**. You can buy a mild narcotic such as codeine with a prescription. Heroin is always illegal.

It is against the law to
smoke marijuana. People
think and act more slowly
when taking the drug.

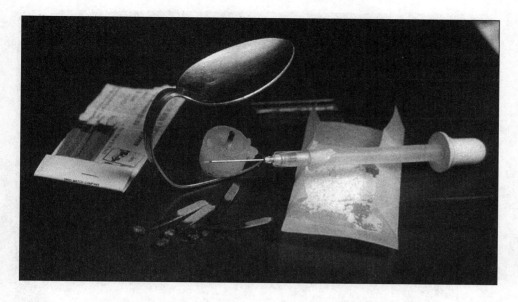

Some people inject heroin into their veins. Many of these people become addicts.

Heroin causes terrible dependence problems. At first heroin makes people feel happy and high. Then people develop emotional and physical dependence on it. They stop feeling high. But they must have the drug to feel normal. Heroin users become **addicts** because their need for heroin is so strong. Heroin addicts have only one goal. That goal is to have enough heroin to feel normal.

Heroin addicts develop tolerance for the drug. They need larger and larger doses of it. Sometimes very large doses kill an addict.

Heroin addicts go through **withdrawal** pains when they do not have the drug. They need medical help to stop using heroin.

Cocaine and **crack** are other illegal drugs. They are **stimulants**. At first they make people feel very happy. But the drugs later make people feel very sad. They use more cocaine and crack to feel happy again. Cocaine and crack abusers have dependence on these drugs. They must have them to feel happy. They develop tolerance for the drugs.

Withdrawal from cocaine and crack is hard. People feel tired and sad. They may become angry easily. They often get into fights. People who abuse cocaine and crack may have a strong need for the drugs for many months after they stop using them.

Addicts are people with such strong dependence on drugs that they cannot stop using them.

Withdrawal is the body's reaction to not having a drug.

Cocaine is an illegal drug that speeds up the nervous system. Its effects last a short time.

Crack is a strong form of cocaine. People smoke crack.

Stimulants are drugs that speed up the body's systems.

Hallucinogens can make people get angry easily.

The Abuse of Hallucinogens and Inhalants

Hallucinogens are drugs that make people see, hear, taste, and smell things differently. Colors and sounds seem different. LSD and PCP are hallucinogens. Angel dust is another name for PCP.

Hallucinogens make people see and hear things that are not real. These drugs can make things look scary and ugly. A string may look like a dangerous snake to a person who is using these drugs.

People feel less pain when they are using hallucinogens. They may burn or cut themselves and not know they are hurt.

Hallucinogens can make people feel very strong and powerful. So they take dangerous risks. Some drug abusers have jumped out of windows. Others become angry easily.

Hallucinogens are different from other drugs. They stay in the body's fat cells for many months. Since the drug stays in the body, it can start to work again many months later. People may see and hear things again that are not real. They may use risk behaviors again.

Hallucinogens can damage the brain. People using hallucinogens sometimes cannot think or speak clearly. They forget things. People develop emotional dependence on these drugs. They feel they must use them. Hallucinogens can cause death.

Inhalants are another group of drugs. You can buy many inhalants in stores. Spray paint, nail polish, airplane glue, and paint remover are inhalants. They become dangerous drugs when people abuse them in order to have pleasant feelings.

At first inhalants can make people feel relaxed and happy. People might feel dizzy later. They often throw up. They can have nosebleeds. People develop emotional dependence on inhalants. They must keep using them to feel good.

People develop tolerance for inhalants. So people must breathe in larger amounts to feel relaxed. Inhalants harm the body. They damage the lungs and the brain. They make the heart beat more slowly. People breathe much more slowly after abusing these drugs. People can die if inhalants make them stop breathing.

Look at the charts on pages 150–153. These charts list other drugs that people often abuse.

People sniff **inhalants** in order to have pleasant feelings.

Some people abuse paint by inhaling it. Inhalants can make you feel dizzy.

If someone asks you to abuse drugs, you can talk to a trusted adult about it.

Saying No to Drugs

Use these refusal skills to say no if someone asks you to abuse drugs.

1. Look at the person and say no. Tell why.
2. Suggest another activity in place of abusing drugs.
3. Walk away if the person pressures you.
4. Tell a parent or trusted adult.

Kelly used refusal skills. Anne invited Kelly to go to a party. Anne and Kelly knew the people at the party would be smoking marijuana. Kelly looked at Anne and said, "No, I won't use marijuana. Let's go to a movie instead." Anne tried to change Kelly's mind. Kelly walked away from Anne. Later that night Kelly talked to her father about what happened.

People who abuse drugs may ask you again and again to try drugs. Drug abusers may tell you that everyone uses drugs. They may say you are not part of the group if you do not use drugs.

Protect yourself from peer pressure to abuse drugs. Remember these four rules.

1. Do not abuse drugs even once. Abusing drugs can ruin your life.
2. Choose friends who do not abuse drugs.

3. Know that real friends do not want you to harm yourself with drugs.
4. Stay away from places where people abuse drugs.

Help for Drug Abusers

It is very hard for most drug abusers to stop abusing drugs. They must really want to stop.

To change their habits, drug abusers must stop using all drugs. When they stop using the drugs, abusers may have withdrawal pains. People often need medical care when they stop abusing drugs. Abusers can get help at drug treatment centers and special **clinics**. People can get information on how to stop abusing drugs from a school nurse or their doctor. They can also call a drug hot line.

Clinics are places where doctors and nurses treat health problems.

Drug abusers should learn new ways to solve problems. They must learn decision-making skills. They need refusal skills to help them say no to drugs.

Feel good about yourself without abusing drugs. By saying no to drugs, you can have a healthier life.

At drug treatment centers, drug abusers learn how to make decisions and solve problems.

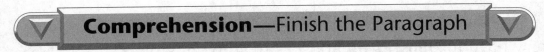

Comprehension—Finish the Paragraph

Use the words in the box to finish each sentence. Write the words you choose on the correct lines.

refusal	no
pressure	abuse

Sometimes people you know will try to get you to _____

drugs. They may use peer _____ to talk you into abusing

drugs. You can use _____ skills to protect yourself. Be sure

to say _____ if someone asks you to abuse drugs.

Vocabulary—Using Vocabulary

Use each word to write a complete sentence about drug abuse.

1. narcotic _____

_____

2. stimulant _____

_____

3. withdrawal _____

_____

4. addicts _____

_____

5. doses _____

_____

6. cancer_____

_____

 Critical Thinking—Categories

Read the words in each group. Decide how they are alike. Find the best title in the box for each group. Write the title on the line beside each group.

inhalants	**drug addicts**	**marijuana**
refusal skills	**heroin**	**hallucinogens**

1. causes lung cancer _____
   makes people forgetful
   slows thinking and movement

2. dependence problems _____
   narcotic
   illegal drug

3. PCP and LSD_____
   cause brain damage
   people see and hear things that are not real

4. can cause nosebleeds _____
   harm the lungs and brain
   spray paint, nail polish, airplane glue

5. dependent on a drug_____
   have poor decision-making skills
   may die from large doses of a drug

6. say no_____
   stay away from people who abuse drugs
   don't go to places where drugs are abused

Alcohol and Health

Think About as You Read

- Why is alcohol a dangerous drug?
- Why do people drink alcohol?
- How can alcoholics be helped?

Alcohol is a dangerous drug. You can say no when people ask you to drink alcohol.

Jason went to a party. Many people were drinking beer. His friends tried to get him to drink some beer. Jason used refusal skills to say no to his friends. Later he left the party. Jason had decided that he would not drink alcohol.

Alcohol Is a Dangerous Drug

More people use alcohol than any other drug. Alcohol comes in many types of drinks. Beer, wine, and liquor have alcohol in them.

Every state has made alcohol illegal for people under a certain age. In the United States, you must be at least 21 years old to buy and use alcohol. Teen-agers who buy alcohol are breaking the law.

When a person drinks alcohol, it quickly goes into the blood. The blood carries alcohol to every cell in the body. Alcohol is a **depressant**. It changes the way the brain works.

Alcohol slows down the messages that the brain sends through the nerves. Alcohol will slow down your thinking. You will not be able to think as clearly. Alcohol will slow down the way your body moves. This can cause you to have accidents. Drunk drivers cause more than half of all car accidents.

There are three main reasons why people abuse alcohol. Some people abuse it because they have low self-esteem. Other people are bored. They think it will be fun to get high on alcohol. Others want their friends who drink alcohol to accept them.

Drunk drivers cause more than half of all car accidents. Don't drink and drive.

Why Is Alcohol Harmful?

Abusing alcohol for a long period of time can harm your physical health. It can damage your brain, your heart, and your digestive system. It can destroy your liver and cause death.

Alcohol abuse harms your social health. People who abuse alcohol cannot work well with others in school or at their jobs. Some people who abuse alcohol get into fights.

Alcohol abuse harms your emotional health. Many people cannot control their feelings when they abuse alcohol. Alcohol stops them from making wise decisions. They are more likely to abuse other family members and friends, too.

Alcohol abuse causes physical and emotional dependence. People can develop tolerance for alcohol. They need to drink larger amounts to feel normal. Withdrawal is very painful.

If a pregnant female drinks, the alcohol can harm the unborn baby. Even small amounts of alcohol can harm the baby. But large amounts can damage the brain, the heart, and the body of an unborn baby.

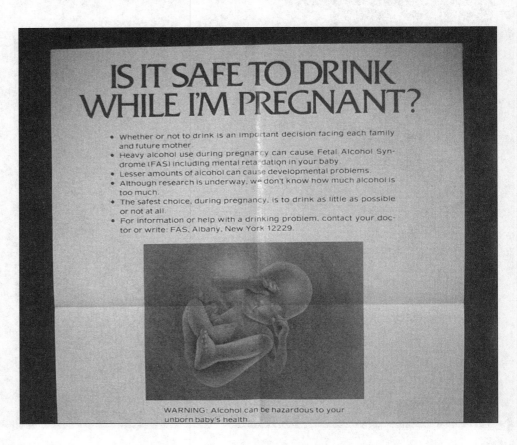

Alcohol can damage the brain, the heart, and the body of an unborn baby.

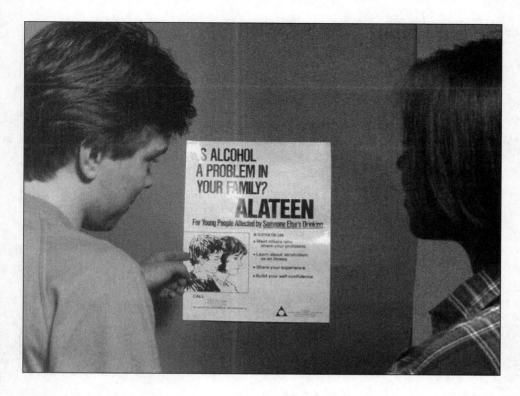

Alateen groups help teen-agers live with family members who are alcoholics.

Understanding and Treating Alcoholism

There are many people who cannot make wise decisions about using alcohol. They abuse alcohol even when it causes problems in their lives. Some cannot stop drinking once they start. These people suffer from the disease of **alcoholism**. They are **alcoholics**. About four million teen-agers have drinking problems.

Here are some signs of alcoholism.

1. The person is often drunk.
2. The person drinks alcohol in the morning.
3. The person does poor work at school or at work.
4. The person drinks secretly.
5. The person forgets many things.
6. The person needs larger amounts of alcohol.

There is no cure for alcoholism. Alcoholics control their disease by not drinking alcohol.

Many alcoholics need help to stop drinking. They need to get help from a doctor or treatment program. Doctors and treatment programs can help alcoholics withdraw from alcohol. Alcoholics also need to learn better ways to solve problems. They need to learn to make wise decisions and use refusal skills.

Alcoholism is a disease in which a person's need to drink alcohol is strong. The person cannot control the need to drink.

95

Teens make wise decisions when they choose friends who do not drink alcohol.

Recovering alcoholics have learned how to stop drinking alcohol.

Alcoholics Anonymous is a group of recovering alcoholics who help each other avoid alcohol.

Recovering alcoholics must never drink alcohol again. They need help from groups like **Alcoholics Anonymous**. Members help each other avoid alcohol. Other groups help teen-agers stop drinking.

Saying No to Alcohol

Alcohol will not be a problem for you if you never use it. It takes only one drink for many people to become alcoholics.

Many teen-agers drink alcohol because their friends do. Teens are making wise decisions when they choose friends who do not drink alcohol.

Anita used refusal skills when her friend Julie asked her to drink beer. Anita said, "No, Julie, I don't drink alcohol. Let's have a soda instead." Julie laughed at Anita and made fun of her decision. Then Julie tried to change Anita's mind. Anita left. She later talked to her mother about what had happened. Anita and her mother felt Anita had made a good decision.

Some decisions are harder to make than others. You are making a wise decision if you never use alcohol. Your decision will help you have good health and wellness.

Vocabulary—Matching

Match the vocabulary word in **Group B** with its definition from **Group A**.
Write the letter of the correct answer on the line.

Group A

_____ 1. This disease cannot be cured, but it can be controlled if the person stops drinking alcohol.

_____ 2. These people often need help from a doctor or treatment center to stop drinking alcohol.

_____ 3. This drug slows down the nervous system.

_____ 4. These people used to drink, but they have learned to say no to alcohol.

_____ 5. The members of this group help each other avoid drinking alcohol.

Group B

a. alcoholics

b. Alcoholics Anonymous

c. alcoholism

d. recovering alcoholics

e. alcohol

Comprehension—Writing About Health

Answer the following question in complete sentences.

What are five signs of alcoholism?

_____

_____

_____

_____

_____

Critical Thinking—Cause and Effect

Read each pair of sentences. Write **Cause** next to the sentence that tells a cause. Write **Effect** next to the sentence that tells an effect.

1. _____ You make wise decisions about alcohol.

   _____ You use refusal skills to say no to beer, wine, and liquor.

2. _____ Alcohol slows down the way the body moves.

   _____ Alcohol is a depressant.

3. _____ A pregnant female chooses not to drink alcohol.

   _____ A pregnant female wants to have a healthy baby.

4. _____ A person has abused alcohol for many years.

   _____ A person has poor physical health.

5. _____ Many alcoholics get help from a doctor or treatment program.

   _____ Many alcoholics cannot stop drinking without help.

6. _____ Alcoholics can control their disease by not drinking.

   _____ There is no cure for alcoholism.

7. _____ The blood carries alcohol.

   _____ Alcohol quickly goes to every cell in the body.

8. _____ A person has a physical and emotional dependence on alcohol.

   _____ A person needs to drink larger amounts of alcohol just to feel normal.

Tobacco and Health

- **Why is tobacco harmful?**
- **How does cigarette smoke hurt people who do not smoke?**
- **Why do people smoke?**

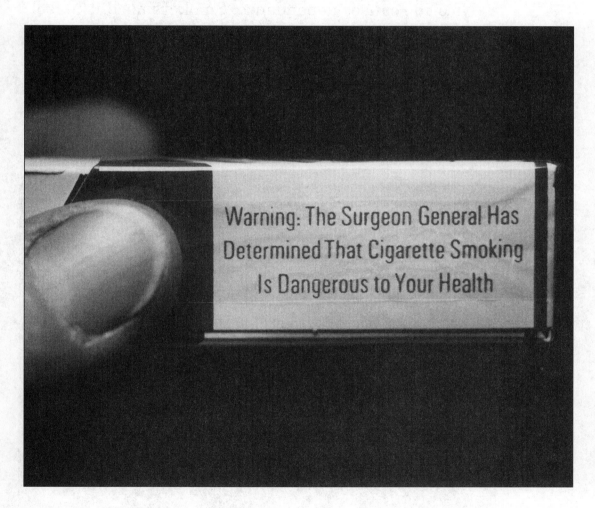

Tobacco is a harmful drug. You can find a warning label on every cigarette box.

Would you spend $400 or more a year on something that could make you very sick? Millions of people do. They spend money to buy cigarettes. They harm their health with tobacco.

How Does Tobacco Hurt People?

More people die each year of health problems caused by the use of tobacco than from any other drug. Most tobacco is smoked in cigarettes. Some people chew, dip, or sniff **smokeless tobacco**. All types of tobacco can harm your health.

There are many dangerous chemicals in tobacco. The most dangerous is **nicotine**. Nicotine is a poison. It is also a stimulant. It makes the heart beat faster. It raises blood pressure. People who use tobacco have more heart attacks and heart diseases than people who do not use tobacco.

Nicotine causes dependence. Smokers need it to feel good. Nicotine makes it hard to stop smoking.

Tobacco can harm the unborn babies of pregnant females who smoke. Nicotine travels through the umbilical cord to the baby. It can cause the unborn baby to be born too early. Pregnant females who smoke often have smaller babies that are less healthy.

Smokeless tobacco is made from tobacco leaves and is chewed, dipped, or sniffed.

Nicotine is a drug in tobacco that causes dependence.

People chew, dip, or sniff smokeless tobacco. All tobacco is harmful to your health.

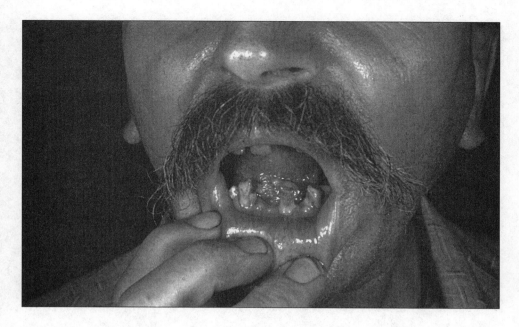

Smoking cigarettes can cause cancer in the mouth. It causes lip, throat, and lung cancer.

Tobacco is harmful in seven other ways.
1. Smokers may have very bad coughs.
2. Smokers become short of breath and feel tired more easily than people who do not smoke.
3. Smokers have more heart and lung diseases than people who do not smoke.
4. Smokers are more likely to get lung cancer.
5. Smokers get more mouth, lip, and throat cancers. They get other cancers more often.
6. Tobacco harms the teeth. It also makes ugly, yellow stains on teeth.
7. Smokers cause more fires in their homes.

Smoking Harms People Who Do Not Smoke

Cigarettes can harm you even if you never smoke. When people smoke cigarettes, tobacco smoke goes into the air. The smoke in the air is **sidestream smoke**. If you are in a room with people who are smoking, you are breathing sidestream smoke. You are a **passive smoker** when you breathe tobacco smoke.

Sidestream smoke is full of dangerous chemicals. People who live or work with smokers have to breathe these dangerous chemicals. Passive smokers develop lung disease and lung cancer more often than people who breathe clean air.

Sidestream smoke is the smoke sent into the air by the burning end of a cigarette, pipe, or cigar.

A **passive smoker** breathes smoke from cigarettes, pipes, or cigars.

Use refusal skills to say no to smoking. You can say, "No. I don't smoke."

Many public places protect people from sidestream smoke. Most offices and restaurants have separate areas for smokers. Many places no longer allow smoking.

Why Do People Use Tobacco?

Each year many people start to smoke. Most of these new smokers are teen-agers.

People may smoke for five different reasons. First, some people smoke because they are copying the behavior of family members who smoke. Second, they think smoking cigarettes will help them deal with stress. Third, some people smoke because of peer pressure. They want to fit in with their friends. Fourth, they want to show that they do not have to listen to others who are against smoking.

The fifth reason many people smoke is that they have low self-esteem. Some cigarette **ads** suggest smoking cigarettes makes you popular or good-looking. People with low self-esteem want to be like the people in the ads. Smoking makes them feel more important, grown up, or better looking.

Ads tell what is special or good about a good or service.

102

Saying No to Tobacco

You know about the dangers of smoking. Here are three reasons to say no to tobacco.

1. It is illegal in the United States to smoke if you are under the age of 18.
2. You want to protect your health.
3. You do not want to waste your money on tobacco.

Saying no to smoking will raise your self-esteem. You will feel good about making a healthy decision. Choose friends who do not use tobacco. They will not ask you to smoke.

Use refusal skills to say no to smoking. The chart on this page shows five ways you can say no to smoking.

People who smoke can stop smoking. The body does get used to not having nicotine. The heart and lungs of a person who quits smoking can become healthier. People who want to stop smoking can ask for help from their doctor or school nurse.

The best way to take care of your health is by saying no to tobacco. You can reach your goal of wellness by not starting to use tobacco.

Saying No to Smoking

A Smoker May Say:	You Can Say:
1. Try a cigarette. These are great.	1. No. I don't use tobacco. OR—No. I don't smoke.
2. Everyone smokes.	2. No. I don't smoke because it is dangerous to my health.
3. Let's go to my house. We can smoke there.	3. No. I don't smoke. Let's go to a movie instead.
4. I don't want to be your friend if you don't smoke.	4. I don't need friends who smoke. I have good friends who don't smoke.
5. I really wish you would try my cigarettes.	5. If you were really my friend, you would not ask me to do something to harm my health.

Vocabulary—Find the Meaning

On the line write the word or words that best complete each sentence.

1. When you breathe another person's tobacco smoke, you are a

   _____ .

   dangerous chemical   **passive smoker**   **member**

2. The dangerous stimulant found in tobacco is _____ .
   nicotine   **cancer**   **healthy**

3. If you are in a smoke-filled room, you are breathing

   _____ .

   refusal skills   **smokeless tobacco**   **sidestream smoke**

4. All types of tobacco, including _____ , can cause
   health problems.
   smokeless tobacco   **family members**   **blood pressure**

5. Cigarette _____ try to make people think that
   smoking will make them more popular or better looking.
   dependence   **ads**   **fires**

Comprehension—Write the Questions

Below and on the next page are the answers for some questions from this
chapter. Read each answer. Then write your own question on the line above
each answer. Use the question words to help you.

1. Why _____
   Smoking is dangerous to pregnant females because it can cause the baby
   to be born early and to be smaller and less healthy.

104

2. How _____

_____

Many public places protect people from sidestream smoke by having
separate areas for smokers or by not allowing smoking.

3. Why _____
It is dangerous to be around people who are smoking because the air will
be filled with dangerous chemicals.

4. What_____
The most dangerous chemical in tobacco is nicotine.

5. Who _____
 A doctor or school nurse can help you stop smoking.

6. How _____
You can reach your goal of wellness by not starting to use tobacco.

▽ Critical Thinking—Fact or Opinion ▽

Read each sentence below. Write **Fact** next to each sentence that tells a fact.
Write **Opinion** next to each sentence that tells an opinion. You should find
four sentences that are opinions.

_____ 1. More people die each year from tobacco use than from any other
drug.

_____ 2. Chewing tobacco is less dangerous than smoking tobacco.

_____ 3. Smoking should be illegal.

_____ 4. Smokers have more heart and lung diseases than people who do
not smoke.

_____ 5. It is easy to quit smoking.

_____ 6. Smoking should not be allowed in any public place.

UNIT 4

Fighting Disease

Modern medicine is helping people live longer, healthier lives. There are medicines that cure many diseases. Other medicines can prevent certain diseases. Doctors today have better tests and tools than in years past for learning what happens inside the body.

While doctors work at finding more cures for diseases, many people are using good health habits to stay well. Washing your hands often, exercising, and eating a healthy diet are a few things you can do to protect yourself from disease.

Have You Ever Wondered?

▼ Some diseases spread quickly from one person to another. How?
▼ A cold is very dangerous for a person with AIDS. Why?
▼ High blood pressure can cause other kinds of heart disease. Which ones?

As you read this unit, think about your own health habits. Learn what you can do to avoid disease and reach the goal of wellness.

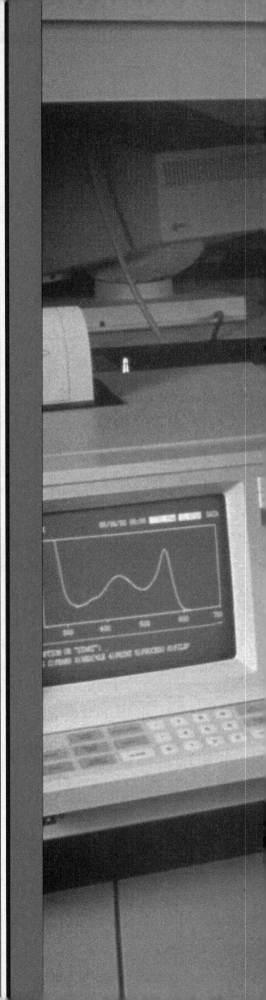

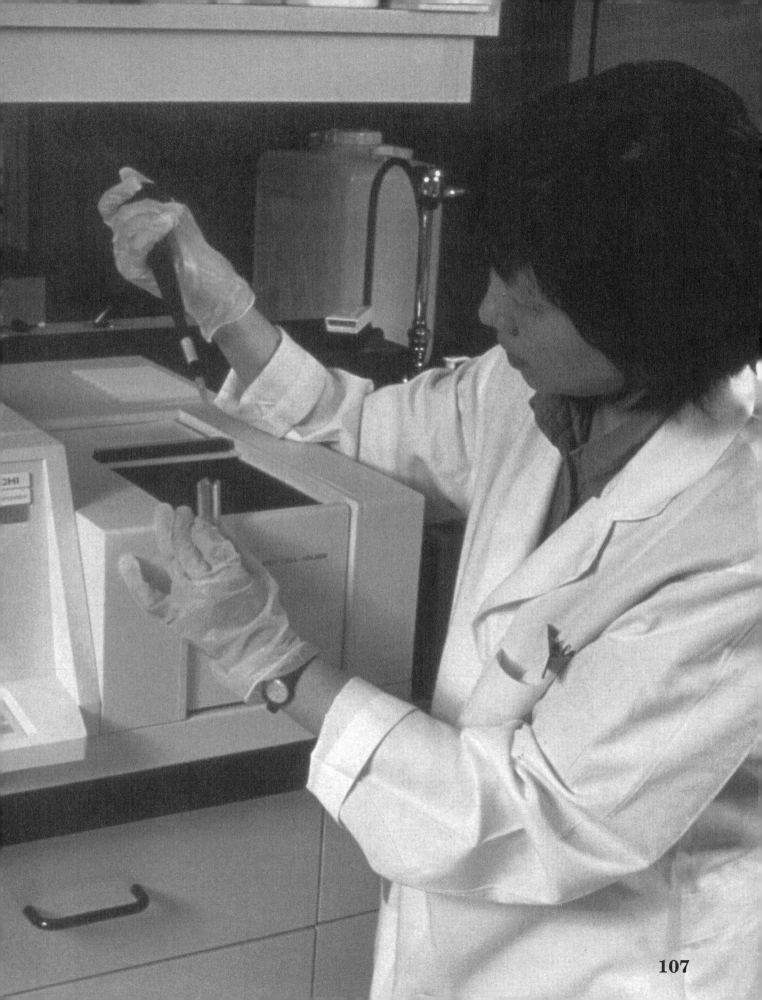

Communicable Diseases

Think About as You Read

- How are communicable diseases spread among people?
- How does the body fight disease?
- How can you avoid disease?

The flu is a communicable disease that spreads quickly during the winter.

A **virus** is a very tiny living thing that causes diseases. A virus can multiply and grow only when it is inside the body's cells.

Every winter a few students in your school may get sick with the flu. Before long the flu may spread to other people in school. A **virus** causes this disease. The flu is one of the many **communicable diseases**. Communicable diseases spread from one person to another. In this chapter you will learn about the causes and treatments of these diseases.

The Cause and Spread of Communicable Diseases

Pathogens cause all communicable diseases. **Bacteria** and viruses are two types of pathogens.

Bacteria **reproduce** quickly inside your body. Antibiotics kill bacteria. As viruses reproduce, they destroy cells. Antibiotics do not kill most viruses.

Communicable diseases are spread in many ways.

1. Touching, hugging, or kissing a sick person can make you sick.
2. Using a sick person's face towel, dish, cup, or other object can make you sick.
3. When a sick person coughs or sneezes, small drops filled with pathogens go into the air. You can get sick from breathing these small drops.
4. You can get sick from eating food that is not cooked or stored in the right way.
5. There are pathogens inside some animals and insects. When animals or insects bite you, those pathogens enter your blood and can cause disease.
6. Flies and other insects often carry pathogens on their bodies. You can get sick from eating food or using dishes and objects that flies have touched.

Pathogens are very tiny living things that cause disease. They are too small to be seen without a microscope.

Bacteria are very tiny living things that have only one cell. Bacteria sometimes cause disease.

To **reproduce** means to make other living things. People reproduce by having babies. Bacteria make more bacteria when they reproduce.

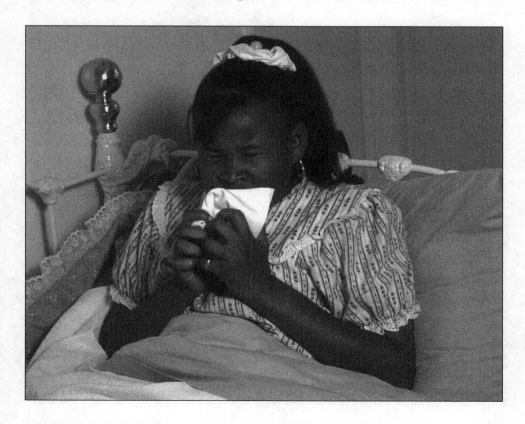

Using a sick person's towels, sheets, and cups can make you sick.

How the Body Fights Disease

Your body has three ways to fight disease. First, unbroken skin keeps most pathogens out of your body. Second, chemicals in your tears, mouth, and stomach kill pathogens. Third, your **immune system** fights disease. Different kinds of white blood cells make up your immune system. One kind of white blood cell makes **antibodies**. Antibodies kill pathogens. Your body makes different antibodies for different diseases.

Vaccines give your body **immunity** to certain diseases. Most vaccines give you immunity that lasts for as long as you live. Other vaccines do not give you lasting immunity. You must take these vaccines again after a number of years have passed. You get most vaccines in shots. You can swallow the polio vaccine.

Common Communicable Diseases

Many different viruses cause colds. Medicines do not cure colds. The best way to prevent colds is by washing your hands often with soap and warm water.

Vaccines are medicines that help the body make antibodies. Vaccines protect you from getting certain diseases.

Immunity means the body can fight off a disease without becoming sick.

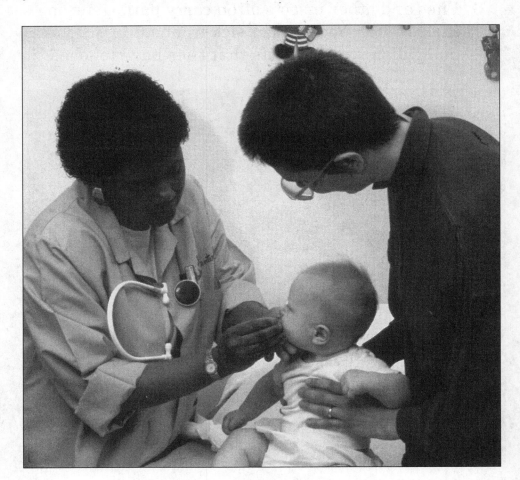

This baby is being given the polio vaccine. This vaccine can be swallowed.

Viruses or bacteria can cause sore throats. **Strep bacteria** cause many sore throats. A doctor will use a **throat culture** to learn which type of sore throat you have. The doctor will give you antibiotics to treat strep throat. Strep throat can cause heart and kidney damage if it is not treated. Always see a doctor if your sore throat lasts more than two days. See a doctor if you have a fever of 101° or higher.

The chart on page 112 provides information about other diseases.

A **throat culture** is the growth of bacteria from the throat. The bacteria grow in a small, closed dish.

Preventing Disease with Good Health Habits

You can protect yourself against communicable diseases. The most important way is by having all the vaccines you need.

Here are eight more health rules that can help you stay well.

1. Wash your hands with soap and warm water before you eat or cook. Wash them after you use the bathroom or change a baby's diaper.
2. Wash cuts with soap and warm water to keep germs out of your body.
3. After preparing raw meat or chicken, wash your hands, knives, and cooking tools with soap and warm water.
4. Use soap and warm water to wash all towels, dishes, and objects after a sick person uses them.
5. Try not to touch and kiss people who have communicable diseases.
6. Cover your nose and mouth with a tissue when you cough or sneeze. Then throw away that used tissue.
7. See a doctor to prevent small health problems from becoming big ones.
8. Take care of your health. Eat healthy foods. Exercise and get enough sleep.

Eating healthy foods helps you protect yourself from communicable diseases.

Good health habits and vaccines can help you avoid communicable diseases. Good health habits and vaccines will help you reach your goal of wellness.

COMMON COMMUNICABLE DISEASES

Disease	Cause	Common Symptoms	Treatment
strep throat	strep bacteria	possible sore throat, fever, swollen glands in the neck	Take antibiotics, drink liquids, and take medicine for pain and body aches.
common cold	more than 100 different viruses	possible sore throat, runny nose, red eyes, cough	Get plenty of bed rest, eat a healthy diet, drink liquids, and take medicine for pain and body aches.
pneumonia	bacteria or viruses	infection and pain in lungs, chest pain, cough, difficulty breathing	Take antibiotics to treat pneumonia caused by bacteria. Get plenty of bed rest, drink fluids, and take medicine for pain and body aches.
flu	viruses	fever, muscle pain, headache, stomachache, sore throat	Get plenty of bed rest, eat a healthy diet, drink fluids, and take medicine for pain and body aches.
hepatitis A	viruses from unclean food or water	liver infection, fever, skin looks yellow, nausea (a sick feeling in the stomach), vomiting (throwing up)	Get plenty of bed rest and eat a healthy diet.
hepatitis B	viruses from infected blood and body fluids	liver infection, fever, skin looks yellow, nausea (a sick feeling in the stomach), vomiting (throwing up)	Get plenty of bed rest and eat a healthy diet.
tuberculosis	bacteria	coughing, coughing up blood, weight loss, feeling very tired, night sweats	Take antibiotics, eat a healthy diet, and get plenty of bed rest.
mononucleosis	viruses	sore throat, swollen glands in the neck, pain in joints, fever, feeling very tired	Eat a healthy diet, get plenty of bed rest, and take medicine for body aches.
chicken pox	viruses	rash, fever, aching muscles	Get plenty of bed rest, drink fluids, take baths, and take medicine for fever and itching.

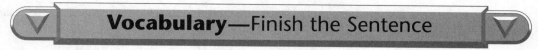

Vocabulary—Finish the Sentence

Choose a word or words in the box to complete each sentence. Write the words on the correct lines.

reproduce	virus	immune system
bacteria	vaccines	antibodies

1. A _____ causes the flu.

2. Viruses and _____ are types of pathogens that can cause communicable diseases.

3. White blood cells make _____ to kill pathogens.

4. Viruses destroy cells as they _____ .

5. White blood cells are part of your _____.

6. You get most _____ in shots.

Comprehension—Write the Questions

Below are the answers for some questions from this chapter. Read each answer. Then write your own question on the line above each answer. Use the question words to help you.

1. Where_____

   Bacteria reproduce in the body.

2. How _____

   Communicable diseases can be spread by touching a sick person.

3. How _____

_____

Unbroken skin helps your body fight disease by keeping pathogens out of your body.

4. What_____

_____

You need a throat culture to find out what type of sore throat you have.

5. How _____

You can prevent many communicable diseases by having all of the vaccines you need.

6. What_____

Cover your nose and mouth with a tissue when you cough or sneeze.

Critical Thinking—Analogies

Use a word or words in the box to finish each sentence.

antibodies	pathogens
strep bacteria	virus

1. Virus is to flu as _____ are to some sore throats.

2. Cold is to communicable disease as _____ is to pathogen.

3. Vaccines are to immunity as _____ are to communicable diseases.

4. The immune system is to fighting disease as _____ are to killing pathogens.

AIDS and STDs

Think About as You Read

- How do people get AIDS?
- How can people protect themselves from STDs and AIDS?
- How does AIDS harm the body?

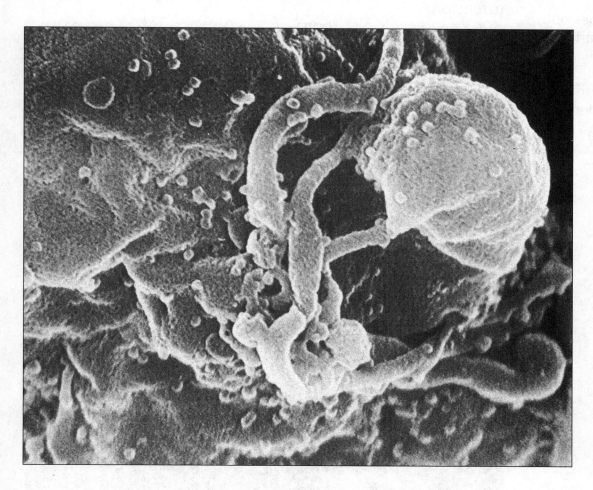

This is the AIDS virus. It attacks and destroys white blood cells.

Magic Johnson is a famous basketball star who has the AIDS virus. Magic Johnson now tells people to protect themselves from AIDS. In this chapter you will learn about AIDS and other sexually transmitted diseases, or STDs.

What Are Sexually Transmitted Diseases?

STDs are communicable diseases. To prevent STDs, avoid intimate sexual behavior.

Some STDs can be treated and cured with antibiotics and other medicines. If STDs are not treated, they can damage your body. You can die from STDs. A pregnant female can pass STDs to her unborn baby.

Chlamydia is the most common STD. One of its **symptoms** is **discharge** from the sex organs. Pregnant females who have chlamydia can pass the disease to their unborn babies. A baby born to a mother with chlamydia may have **pneumonia** and eye infections.

Learn about four STDs from the chart on page 117. Many people do not have symptoms until their bodies are badly damaged. Infected people can spread their disease to others.

Chlamydia is an STD that is caused by bacteria.

Symptoms are signs of a disease.

Discharge comes out of an infected part of the body.

Pneumonia is an infection of the lungs.

Teens who date can protect themselves from STDs by choosing abstinence.

FOUR SEXUALLY TRANSMITTED DISEASES

Disease	Pathogen	Symptoms	Treatment
chlamydia	bacteria	Symptoms can appear 5 to 12 days after infection. At times there are no symptoms. Sometimes there is discharge from the sex organs. If a person with the disease is not treated, the person may not be able to reproduce.	antibiotics
genital herpes	virus	Symptoms can appear 2 to 12 days after infection. Symptoms include painful blisters, burning, and redness of sex organs. Sometimes there are no symptoms. Pregnant females can infect their unborn babies during birth.	no cure
gonorrhea	bacteria	Symptoms can appear 2 to 9 days after infection. Females often have no symptoms. Males may feel pain when they urinate. Males may have discharge from their sex organ. Pregnant females can infect their unborn babies during birth. The disease can cause a person to be unable to reproduce.	antibiotics
syphilis	bacteria	Syphilis has four stages if it is not treated. •*Stage 1*. Symptoms appear about 3 weeks after infection. A painless sore appears on the sex organs. The sore disappears in about 3 weeks. •*Stage 2*. Symptoms begin 6 weeks to 6 months later. The person has rash and fever for several weeks. The rash and fever will disappear without treatment. •*Stage 3*. There are no symptoms for 5 to 20 years. •*Stage 4*. Bacteria attack the body organs. The disease can cause blindness, brain damage, or heart disease. A person with syphilis can die at this stage. Babies of pregnant females who have syphilis may be born dead, or they may die shortly after birth.	Antibiotics can cure syphilis during stages 1, 2, and 3.

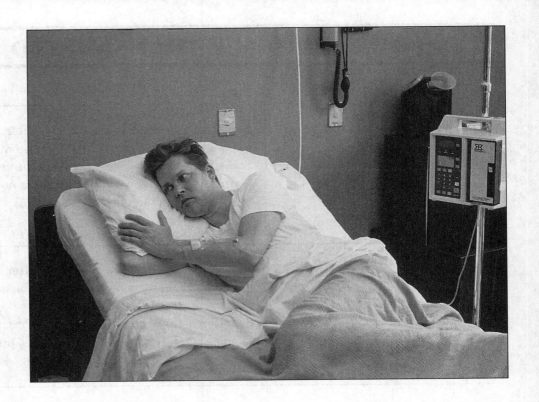

People who are sick with AIDS are very sick. Their immune systems cannot fight germs.

What Is AIDS?

AIDS stands for acquired immune deficiency syndrome. AIDS is always caused by the **HIV virus**. Once the virus enters your body, you are infected for the rest of your life. There is no cure at this time for AIDS. Most people who get sick with AIDS will die.

The HIV virus lives in blood and fluids from the sex organs. The HIV virus kills special white blood cells called T-helper cells. Your immune system cannot fight other diseases without these T-helper cells. People who are sick with AIDS die because their immune systems cannot fight germs and disease.

There is a big difference between having the HIV virus in your body and being sick with AIDS. People who are sick with AIDS are very ill. But most people who get AIDS have the HIV virus in their bodies for 8 to 11 years before they become sick. During this time people who have the HIV virus may look and feel fine. Most people do not even know they have the HIV virus. But they can spread the virus to many people. Most people who have the HIV virus will one day get sick with AIDS and later die.

118

The Three Stages of AIDS

There are three stages of the AIDS disease. During the first stage, the HIV virus enters the body. This stage can last as long as 11 years. People may feel fine. But the virus is slowly destroying the body's T-helper cells. The immune system becomes weak.

During stage two people may still feel fine most of the time. But they will get more infections. One of these diseases is a kind of pneumonia. People also lose weight during this stage.

During stage three the immune system no longer works. People who are sick with AIDS often have fever. They feel very tired and weak. They no longer look well because they have lost far too much weight. Many people who are sick with AIDS get a skin cancer that causes ugly purple marks. Some people who are sick with AIDS lose their hair. They may get skin sores. Many people who are sick with AIDS will die in about two years.

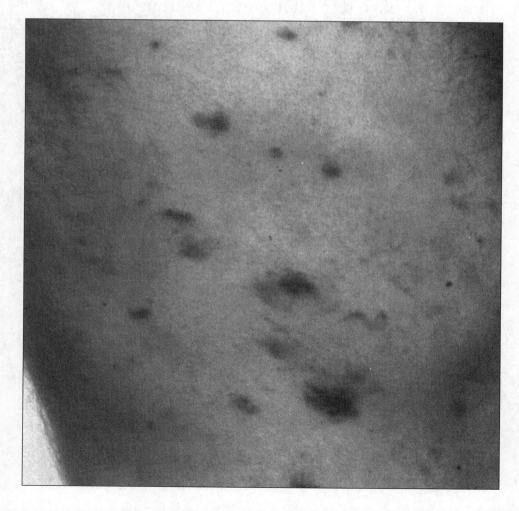

Many people with AIDS get this kind of skin cancer. It causes ugly purple marks.

Getting AIDS and Testing for AIDS

Most people get AIDS through intimate sexual behavior with an infected person. About one fourth of the people with the HIV virus are drug abusers. They get AIDS by sharing drug needles with an infected person. Pregnant females with the HIV virus can pass the HIV virus to their babies. About one third of these babies will get AIDS and later die. Teen-agers who use these risk behaviors can get AIDS.

The chart on this page lists risk behaviors that can cause you to get AIDS. It also lists safe behaviors that never spread AIDS.

If you use any of the risk behaviors, you should have an AIDS blood test. You can learn if you have the HIV virus. You should go for a blood test three months after you think you were infected. People who think or know they have the virus should not spread it to others.

You can find out from your school nurse or doctor where to get an AIDS test and counseling. Health clinics also have this information. Testing is **confidential** or **anonymous**. You can also learn about testing and counseling by calling the AIDS hot line in your town or city. You can also call 1-800-342-AIDS.

Confidential means secret.

Anonymous means someone whose name is not known.

How AIDS Is Spread

Risk Behaviors:

1. You can get AIDS by having intimate sexual behavior with a person who has the HIV virus.

2. You can get AIDS by sharing drug needles with an infected person.

3. Pregnant females with the HIV virus pass the disease to their unborn babies.

Safe Behaviors:

1. You cannot get AIDS by touching, hugging, kissing, or shaking hands with a person with AIDS.

2. You cannot get AIDS by sharing cups, towels, and other objects that were used by a person with AIDS.

3. You cannot get AIDS from animal or insect bites.

4. You cannot get AIDS by using the same bathroom that is used by a person with AIDS.

5. You cannot get AIDS from giving blood to a blood bank.

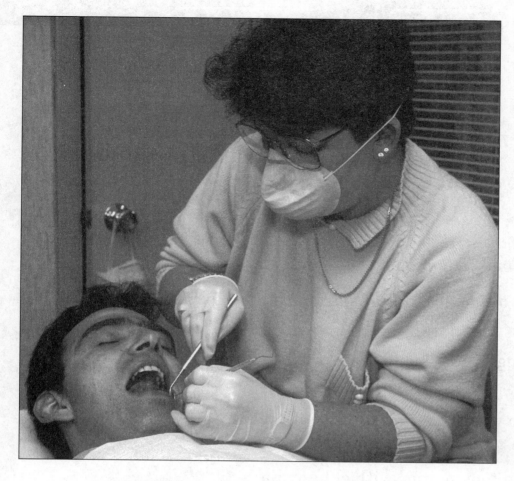

Dentists and health care workers should wear latex gloves when they treat you.

Protecting Yourself from AIDS

These rules will prevent you from getting AIDS.
1. Do not have intimate sexual behavior.
2. Say no to drugs.
3. Do not share needles that are used to **pierce** ears or make tattoos.
4. Always wear **latex** gloves if you must touch other people's blood.
5. Ask your dentist and other health care workers to wear latex gloves when treating you.

Refusal skills can help you say no to intimate sexual behavior. You can say, "I am not ready for intimate sexual behavior." Or you might say, "I believe in waiting until I am married to have intimate sexual behavior." Always say no to risk behaviors that can spread AIDS.

Protect yourself from AIDS and STDs. This can help you have a long, healthy life.

Pierce means to make a hole in something. Many people pierce their ears and wear earrings in the holes.

Latex is a strong, stretchy material like rubber.

121

Using What You Learned

Vocabulary—Matching

Match the vocabulary word in **Group B** with its definition from **Group A**.
Write the letter of the correct answer on the line.

Group A

_____ 1. This is the most common STD.

_____ 2. This comes out of an infected part of the body.

_____ 3. AIDS testing that is kept secret is called this.

_____ 4. You need to wear this type of glove if you must touch other people's blood.

_____ 5. A baby born to a mother with chlamydia can have this infection of the lungs.

Group B

a. discharge

b. pneumonia

c. chlamydia

d. confidential

e. latex

Comprehension—True or False

Write **True** next to each sentence that is true. Write **False** next to each sentence that is false. There are two false sentences.

_____ 1. The AIDS disease has four stages.

_____ 2. You can get AIDS from having intimate sexual behavior with someone who has AIDS.

_____ 3. Pregnant females can infect their unborn babies with AIDS.

_____ 4. The HIV virus helps special white blood cells called T-helper cells.

On the lines below, rewrite the two false sentences to make them true.

_____

_____

_____

Critical Thinking—Drawing Conclusions

Read the paragraph. Then use the six steps to decide what to do about AIDS. Write a complete sentence to answer each question.

You have a friend who has AIDS. You enjoy spending time with this friend. But your other friends do not want you to be around this friend. They are afraid that you will get AIDS, too.

Step 1. What is the problem?

_____

Step 2. What are two ways to solve the problem?

_____

_____

Step 3. What is one consequence, or result, for each choice listed in Step 2?

_____

Step 4. Which choice do you think is best?

_____

Step 5. What can you do to put your decision into action?

_____

Step 6. Think about your decision. Why was this the best choice for you?

_____

Other Diseases

Think About as You Read

- **What are the signs of a heart attack?**
- **What happens during an asthma attack?**
- **What health habits help prevent disease?**

This teen has a food allergy to pizza. He became sick when he ate the pizza.

An **allergy** causes a person to have a runny or stuffy nose, have breathing problems, or have other health problems. An allergy can be caused by food, dust, plants, animals, chemicals, or other things that do not bother many other people.

Kevin and his friends bought a pizza for lunch. Kevin knew he should not eat pizza because he has an **allergy** to milk. He decided to eat the pizza anyway. A short time later, Kevin got pains in his stomach.

An allergy is a **noncommunicable disease**. A noncommunicable disease does not spread from one person to another. Pathogens do not cause noncommunicable diseases. Problems inside the body cause noncommunicable diseases. In this chapter you will learn about some noncommunicable diseases.

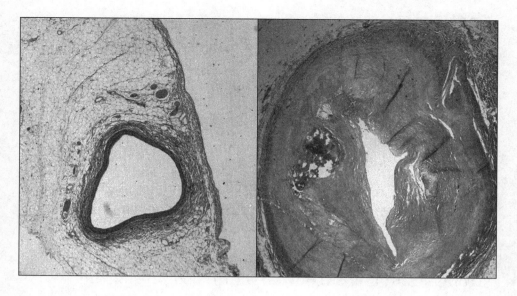

The left artery is healthy. The right artery is blocked with cholesterol.

Cardiovascular Diseases

High blood pressure and **atherosclerosis** are diseases that affect the heart and arteries. These diseases can also lead to two very dangerous cardiovascular diseases, heart attack and **stroke**.

High blood pressure can be caused by many factors. Smoking, stress, and being overweight can greatly increase your blood pressure. Eating foods that are high in fat and salt is another cause of high blood pressure. It is important to have your blood pressure checked regularly. Your doctor can help you find ways to lower your blood pressure if it is too high.

Atherosclerosis is a buildup of **cholesterol** and fats on the inside walls of arteries. Over many years this buildup can cause arteries to become very narrow. The heart must pump much harder to send blood through these arteries. A person with atherosclerosis is at high risk for having a heart attack or a stroke.

A heart attack can happen if an artery becomes so narrow that blood stops flowing to part of the heart. The cells in that part of the heart die. A symptom of a heart attack may be pains in the chest, arms, neck, sholders, or jaw. Dizzy feelings, sweating, difficulty in breathing, and a sick feeling in the stomach are other possible symptoms. A person with any of these symptoms should be taken to a hospital right away.

A **stroke** is a disease that damages the brain. It happens when blood cannot flow through a blocked artery to the brain.

Cholesterol is a fatty substance found in the blood. It can build up inside arteries and cause heart disease.

125

A stroke is a brain attack. It can occur if an artery in the brain bursts or becomes blocked. Nerve cells in part of the brain die because they cannot get oxygen. After a stroke a person may not be able to walk or talk.

Follow these five rules to help lower your risk of getting cardiovascular diseases.

1. Avoid smoking. Smoking greatly increases your risk of getting cardiovascular diseases.

2. Maintain your ideal weight. Being overweight causes your heart to work much harder.

3. Exercise regularly. Exercise makes your heart stronger and helps to lower your blood pressure.

4. Eat foods that are low in salt, fat, and cholesterol.

5. Avoid stress. Stress can increase your blood pressure and cause you to use risk behaviors.

Allergies and Asthma

More than 35 million Americans have allergies. Certain **allergens** cause allergies. The allergens may be foods, animals, plants, dust, or chemicals. Some allergies cause a person to have red eyes, a stuffy nose, or other health problems.

Allergens are any things to which people have allergies.

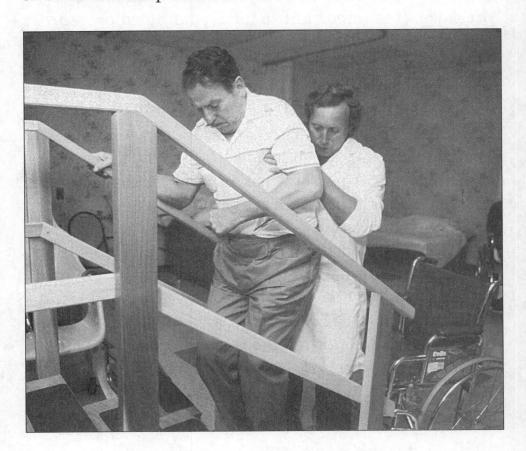

Some people cannot walk after a stroke. Medical care can help them learn to walk again.

126

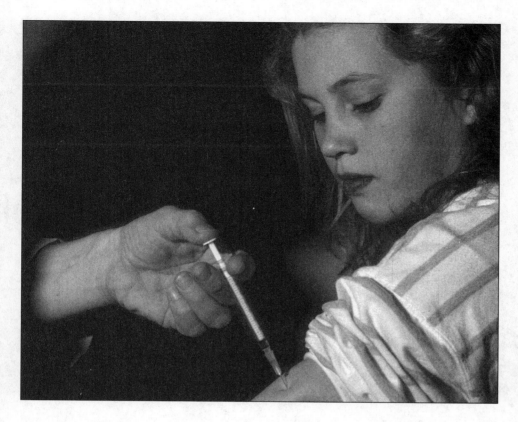

Shots can treat some allergies. The shots reduce the symptoms of allergies.

A doctor can treat allergies. Allergies cannot be cured. Your doctor can help you learn which allergens, if any, are a problem for you. Try to avoid those allergens. If you have an allergy to milk, as Kevin does, avoid all foods with milk. Your doctor can give you medicine for allergies to help you feel more comfortable. Shots can treat some allergies. The shots will reduce the symptoms of allergies.

Asthma is a lung disease. Asthma bothers millions of people. There are tiny tubes in your lungs that carry air to the air sacs. During an asthma attack, the tubes in the lungs become tight and narrow. Air cannot easily move in and out of these tight, narrow tubes. A person with asthma has a hard time breathing. The person coughs a lot during an attack. Allergies or infections cause most asthma attacks.

There is no cure for asthma. Sometimes people's asthma becomes less of a problem when a doctor treats their allergies. Different kinds of medicines can control asthma. All people with asthma need to be under the care of a doctor.

Diabetes

Diabetes is another noncommunicable disease. The body of a person with diabetes cannot use sugar in normal ways. The hormone **insulin** helps the body digest sugar. In some people with diabetes, the body does not make enough insulin. In other people who have diabetes, the body cannot use insulin to digest sugar.

Diabetes has two main symptoms. People often feel very thirsty. They also need to urinate often.

Diabetes can be controlled. People with diabetes can live a long life. They can control diabetes by exercising and eating a special diet. They may need to lose weight. Some people who have diabetes must take insulin shots. Sometimes people take pills to control diabetes.

Have your blood pressure checked at least once a year.

Fiber is a nutrient from plant foods that helps the body remove wastes. Fiber is not digested and used by the body cells.

Protecting Yourself from Disease

Choose healthy behaviors that protect your health. These eight rules can help you prevent many diseases.

1. Do not smoke.
2. Exercise at least three times a week.
3. Eat a diet that is high in **fiber**. Your diet should be low in fat, sugar, salt, and cholesterol. Avoid red meat, egg yolks, and fried foods.
4. Have your blood pressure checked at least once each year.
5. Get enough sleep.
6. Learn how to live with stress. Talk about your feelings with people you trust. Stress weakens your immune system. Stress also makes your blood vessels become narrower.
7. Wash your hands often with soap and warm water.
8. Take a bath or shower every day.

Healthy behaviors help you live with less disease. Choose healthy behaviors to reach your goal of wellness.

Comprehension—Writing About Health

Answer the following question in complete sentences.

What are four healthy behaviors that help prevent many diseases?

_____

_____

_____

_____

_____

Vocabulary—Find the Meaning

On the line write the word or words that best complete each sentence.

1. A _____ disease cannot be spread from one person to another.

   communicable   **noncommunicable**   **sexually transmitted**

2. The hormone _____ helps the body digest sugar.

   insulin   **fiber**   **cholesterol**

3. Atherosclerosis can cause a _____ or a heart attack.

   pathogen   **chemical**   **stroke**

4. You can help prevent diseases by eating a diet that is high in

   _____ .

   fiber   **smoke**   **allergens**

5. A build-up of _____ narrows the inside of your arteries.

asthma   **insulin**   **cholesterol**

Critical Thinking—Fact or Opinion

Read each sentence below. Write **Fact** next to each sentence that tells a fact. Write **Opinion** next to each sentence that tells an opinion. You should find six sentences that are opinions.

_____ 1. People with diabetes often feel thirsty and need to urinate.

_____ 2. Finding a friend with whom you can talk is the hardest part of learning to live with stress.

_____ 3. The most painful part of having a heart attack is the chest pains.

_____ 4. The tubes in the lungs become tight and narrow when a person has an asthma attack.

_____ 5. It is easy to protect yourself from diseases.

_____ 6. Pathogens do not cause noncommunicable diseases.

_____ 7. It is easier to live with allergies than any other noncommunicable disease.

_____ 8. Smoking and stress can lead to high blood pressure.

_____ 9. Stress weakens your immune system and makes your blood vessels narrow.

_____ 10. Chest pains are one sign that a person might be having a heart attack.

_____ 11. Getting enough sleep is the best way to avoid diseases.

_____ 12. A stroke is the worst kind of cardiovascular disease.

Cancer

Think About as You Read

- What are the seven signs of cancer?
- How do doctors treat cancer?
- How can you avoid getting cancer?

This person had cancer. She was treated and cured. She is healthy today.

Gina is 15 years old. She knows she is lucky because she is healthy today. Six years ago Gina had a type of cancer called **leukemia**. Gina has had many treatments. Now she is cured. In this chapter you will learn how to treat and prevent cancer.

Understanding Cancer

Cancer cells reproduce faster than normal cells. Cancer cells damage your body's healthy cells and organs.

Leukemia causes the body to make too many white blood cells that are not normal. These white blood cells cannot fight germs.

A **tumor** is a lump that grows in the body. A tumor can be made of normal cells or cancer cells.

A **sunscreen lotion** blocks the sun's harmful rays from damaging your skin.

SPF stands for sun protection factor. An SPF number tells how much protection a sunscreen provides.

Cancer cells often grow into a **tumor**. A tumor can grow in any part of the body. Cancer cells can break away from the tumor. The blood carries cancer cells to other parts of the body. The cancer cells form new tumors in different parts of the body. A person becomes very sick when cancer spreads throughout the body.

Most lumps in the body are not cancer. You should always have your doctor check all lumps.

Doctors can cure some cancer. They must find and treat small tumors before the tumors grow and spread throughout the body.

Three Types of Cancer

There are many types of cancer. All cancers are noncommunicable diseases. Skin cancer, lung cancer, and leukemia are three common types of cancer.

Spending too much time in the sun for many years causes skin cancers. Always use a **sunscreen lotion** when you are in the sun. The lotion should have an **SPF** number of 15 or higher. When you are in the sun, wear a hat and lightweight clothes to protect yourself. Doctors can cure most skin cancers that are found early.

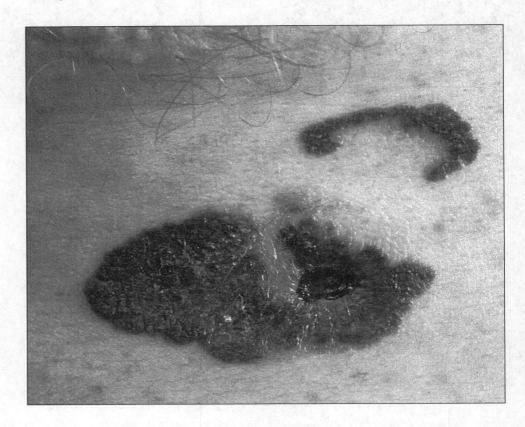

Spending too much time in the sun can cause skin cancers. How can you protect your skin?

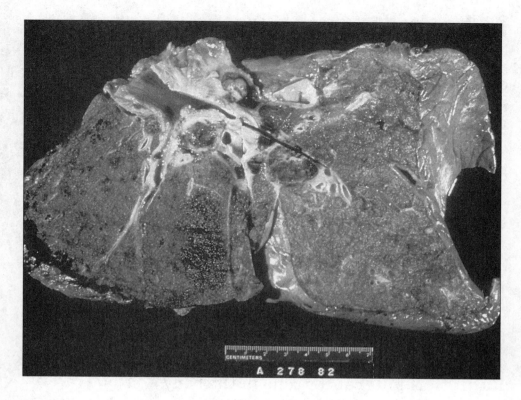

This lung belonged to a smoker. The lung cancer was caused by cigarette smoking.

Lung cancer kills more Americans than any other cancer. Smoking causes most cases of lung cancer. Lung cancer is very hard to cure.

Leukemia is the most common cancer in children. Adults also get this disease. There are many ways to treat this cancer. Most children can be cured of leukemia.

Seven Warning Signs of Cancer

The American Cancer Society tells people to look for the seven signs of cancer. See your doctor if you have any of these warning signs for more than two weeks.

1. A sore on any part of the body does not heal.
2. A small or large lump is in the breast or any part of the body.
3. A **mole** or wart changes in size, shape, or color.
4. You have a cough or a hoarse voice.
5. There is a change in your **bowel** or bladder habits.
6. You have difficulty swallowing or a sick feeling in the stomach because your body cannot digest food.
7. You have unusual bleeding or discharge.

A **mole** is a black or brown spot on the skin.

The intestine is also called the **bowel**. Food passes from the stomach into your bowels. Solid waste leaves your body when you have a bowel movement.

133

Finding, Treating, and Preventing Cancer

Males between the ages of 15 and 34 sometimes get cancer in their testes. Males should check their testes once a month. They should see a doctor if they think there are changes in their testes.

Females can get cancer in their breasts. The disease can be cured by removing the tumor. Females should check their breasts for lumps once a month. The best time to do this is soon after menstruation has stopped.

Some females get cancer in their reproductive organs. A **Pap test** can find this type of cancer. Females should have a Pap test once a year.

Doctors start a person's cancer treatment soon after the cancer is found. **Surgery** removes tumors made of cancer cells that are in small areas of the body. **Radiation** kills cancer cells in the body. **Chemotherapy** kills cancer cells that might have spread throughout the body. People are cured when they have no sign of cancer for five years.

Here are six ways to avoid getting cancer.

1. Do not smoke or use tobacco.
2. Do not breathe dangerous chemicals.
3. Eat foods that are high in fiber and low in fat.
4. Eat many kinds of fruits and vegetables.
5. Do not drink alcohol.
6. Wear a sunscreen lotion in the sun.

You can protect yourself against cancer. Having good health habits will help you.

Surgery is the use of medical tools to cut and repair the body.

Radiation is a treatment for cancer. Very strong rays are aimed at cancer cells to kill them.

Chemotherapy is the treatment of cancer with powerful medicines.

Say no to cigarettes. You will help protect yourself from lung cancer.

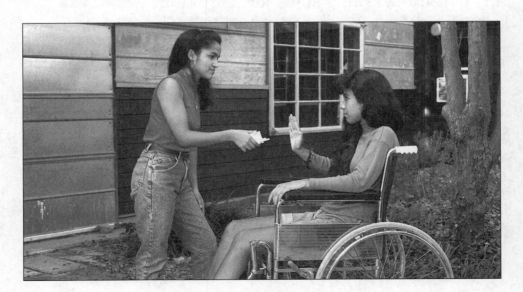

134

Vocabulary—Finish the Sentence

Choose a word or words in the box to complete each sentence. Write the words on the correct lines.

mole	tumor	Pap test
surgery	chemotherapy	sunscreen lotion

1. A _____ is a lump in the body made of normal cells or cancer cells.

2. You should wear _____ to protect your skin from the sun's harmful rays.

3. Tumors that are made of cancer cells can be removed from small areas of the body using _____ .

4. A _____ can be used to find cancer in a female's reproductive organs.

5. Radiation and _____ kill cancer cells in the body.

6. A _____ is a brown or black spot on the skin.

Comprehension—Write the Answer

Write an answer in a complete sentence to each question.

1. What happens when cancer cells break away from a tumor?

_____

_____

2. Why shouldn't you spend too much time in the sun?

_____

3. What is the most common cancer in children?

_____

4. What should you do if you think you have cancer?

_____

5. Where do males sometimes get cancer?

_____

Critical Thinking—Categories

Read the words in each group. Decide how they are alike. Find the best title in the box for each group. Write the title on the line beside each group.

cancer treatments	types of cancer
prevent cancer	signs of cancer

1. skin cancer _____
   lung cancer
   leukemia

2. sore that won't heal _____
   change in a mole or wart
   small or large lump

3. surgery_____
   radiation
   chemotherapy

4. wear a sunscreen lotion_____
   eat foods that are high in fiber and low in fat
   don't smoke or use tobacco

Understanding and Treating Disease

Think About as You Read

- **What can doctors learn from blood tests and urine tests?**
- **How does a doctor make a diagnosis?**
- **What new ways of doing surgery help people?**

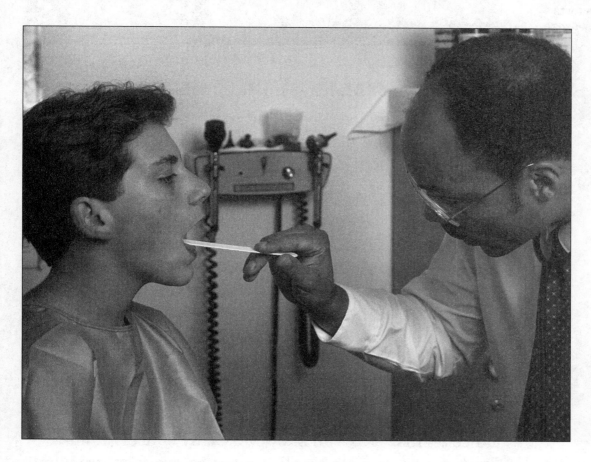

A doctor will use different tests to learn what is causing this patient's sore throat.

Each year scientists invent new medicines to treat disease. Doctors must know why a person is sick to order the correct medicine. Better ways of making a **diagnosis** help doctors learn why people are sick. In this chapter you will learn about the diagnosis and treatment of disease.

A **diagnosis** is the name given to a disease or health condition. A doctor makes a diagnosis after examining and studying the symptoms of a patient.

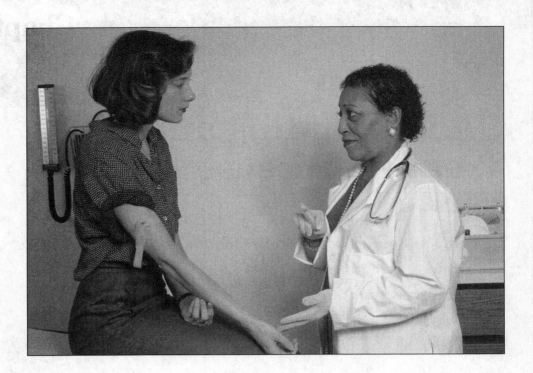

Blood tests show the health of the blood. These tests can show many diseases and allergies.

Many Ways of Making a Diagnosis

Doctors use blood tests and urine tests to make a diagnosis. Blood tests show the health of the blood. These tests show many allergies and diseases. They also show other problems. Urine tests show if a person has an infection. Sugar in the urine is a sign of diabetes. Blood in the urine is a sign of infection or disease.

Doctors use a special machine to record a person's heartbeat. The machine records on a sheet of paper the pattern of the heartbeat. This record is a **cardiogram**. Sometimes the pattern on the cardiogram is not normal. This is a sign of heart disease.

Doctors use x-rays to get information about bones and teeth. A **mammogram** helps doctors find breast cancer. This x-ray can show very tiny cancer tumors. Doctors can remove small tumors before they grow and spread.

Ultrasound helps doctors learn what is happening inside the body. Doctors use ultrasound to learn about the health of the body's organs. Ultrasound helps doctors find tumors. It helps doctors learn about the health of an unborn baby.

Ultrasound is the use of sound waves to outline the shape of a person's body parts.

Treatments Using Medicine

Today doctors use many different antibiotics to cure diseases. Scientists are always making new antibiotics. They are also working on new drugs to cure cancer.

Years ago doctors gave all medicines in pills, liquids, or shots. Now some people wear medicine patches on their skin. The medicine slowly goes through the skin and into the blood. Medicine patches help many people who have heart disease.

Surgery to Treat Disease

Organ **transplants** save the lives of many people with diseased organs. Sometimes a person's heart, kidneys, or other organs are so diseased that the person will die. Doctors may use surgery to remove a diseased organ. Then they replace that organ with a healthy organ from a **donor**.

Transplants are body parts from a healthy person that replace the diseased parts of another person.

A **donor** is the person from whom body parts are taken to use in a transplant. A donor can be dead or living.

This healthy kidney will be given to a person who has a diseased kidney.

Rejection can be a problem for a person who has an organ transplant. The body's immune system attacks the organ from the donor. There are new drugs to stop rejection of transplants. These drugs are helping people with transplants live for many years.

Bypass surgery helps many people who have narrow arteries. Their arteries are blocked with cholesterol. Doctors can do bypass surgery on a person to prevent a heart attack. During surgery doctors remove a short piece of a blood vessel from the chest or leg of the person. Doctors then attach that piece to the blocked artery. The blood flows more easily through the new blood vessels. The heart gets the blood it needs. Then it does not have to work as hard.

Sometimes diseases or accidents destroy parts of the body. Doctors now replace diseased joints with **artificial** ones. They can replace a diseased lens of the eye with an artificial one.

The diagnosis and treatment of disease improves every year. You can learn about the newest ways by watching the news on TV. You can also learn about them by reading the newspaper. This information can help you choose the best health care. Your decisions can help you reach the goal of wellness.

Artificial describes something that is made by people.

Some doctors do laser surgery. Strong beams of light cut and repair the body.

Comprehension—Finish the Paragraph

Use the words in the box to finish each sentence. Write the words you choose on the correct lines.

teeth	organs	urine
diagnosis	pattern	

Doctors make a _____ by using different tests and

machines. Blood tests and _____ tests can tell a

doctor if a person has allergies, an infection, or a disease. Doctors use a

machine to see the _____ of a person's heartbeat.

They take x-rays to check a person's _____ and bones.

Doctors use an ultrasound to find out about the health of the body's

_____ .

Vocabulary—Using Vocabulary

Use each word to write a complete sentence about understanding and treating disease.

1. transplants _____

_____

2. mammogram _____

_____

3. cardiogram _____

_____

4. ultrasound _____

_____

Read each pair of sentences. Write **Cause** next to the sentence that tells a cause. Write **Effect** next to the sentence that tells an effect.

1. _____ Many people suffer from disease.

_____ Scientists invent new medicines.

2. _____ Your doctor thinks you might have a bladder infection.

_____ Your doctor gives you a urine test.

3. _____ The pattern on the cardiogram is not normal.

_____ A person has heart disease.

4. _____ A female has breast cancer.

_____ The doctor removes the tumors from the breast before the tumors grow and spread.

5. _____ The doctor worries about the health of a pregnant female's unborn baby.

_____ The doctor uses ultrasound on the pregnant female.

6. _____ You want to make the best health care choices that you can.

_____ You read newspapers to learn more about health care.

7. _____ A person has bypass surgery.

_____ A person's arteries are blocked with cholesterol.

8. _____ Disease has destroyed a joint in the body.

_____ The joint is replaced with an artificial one.

abstinence page 46
Abstinence is choosing not to do something. People may choose not to have intimate sexual behavior.

acceptance page 38
Acceptance is the feeling that others like you and enjoy being with you.

addicts page 85
Addicts are people with such strong dependence on drugs that they cannot stop using them.

adrenal glands page 31
Your adrenal glands make a hormone that helps the body handle fear and danger.

adrenaline page 31
The adrenal glands make adrenaline, a hormone that helps the body in times of danger.

ads page 102
Ads tell what is special about a good or service.

AIDS page 46
AIDS is a disease in which the body cannot fight germs. AIDS can be spread through body fluids. There is no cure for AIDS.

air sacs page 20
Air sacs are tiny bags of air in the lungs. Air sacs are surrounded by blood vessels.

alcoholics page 95
Alcoholics are people who have the disease of alcoholism.

Alcoholics Anonymous page 96
Alcoholics Anonymous is a group of recovering alcoholics who help each other avoid alcohol.

alcoholism page 95
Alcoholism is a disease in which a person's need to drink alcohol is strong. The person cannot control the need.

allergens page 126
Allergens are any things to which people have allergies.

allergy page 124
An allergy causes a person to have a runny or stuffy nose, have breathing problems, or have other health problems. An allergy can be caused by food, dust, plants, animals, chemicals, or other things that do not bother many other people.

anonymous page 120
Anonymous means someone whose name is not known.

antibiotics page 75
Antibiotics are medicines that can kill germs that cause disease.

antibodies page 110
Antibodies are made by the white blood cells to destroy pathogens.

arteries page 13
Arteries are blood vessels that carry blood away from the heart to other parts of the body.

artificial page 140
Artificial describes something that is made by people.

asbestos page 22
Asbestos is used to make a building material that does not burn. Asbestos was used in the ceilings or walls of older buildings.

asthma page 127
Asthma is a lung disease. A person who has asthma has a hard time breathing air in and out of the lungs.

atherosclerosis page 125
Atherosclerosis is a disease in which cholesterol builds up on the inside walls of the arteries.

bacteria page 109
Bacteria are very tiny living things that have only one cell. Bacteria sometimes cause disease.

bladder page 23
Your bladder is the organ that holds urine until it leaves the body.

blood pressure page 15
Blood pressure is the force of your blood as it moves against the walls of the arteries or heart.

blood vessels page 13
Blood vessels are the different kinds of tubes that carry blood throughout the body.

bowel page 133
The intestine is also called the bowel. Food passes from the stomach into your bowels. Solid waste leaves your body when you have a bowel movement.

bypass surgery page 140
Bypass surgery is used to make new blood vessels for carrying blood to the heart. The new blood vessels are made from blood vessels in the legs or chest.

calcium page 8
Calcium is a mineral that the body needs for strong bones and teeth.

cancer page 84
Cancer is a disease in which unhealthy cells multiply too rapidly and destroy body parts.

capillaries page 13
Capillaries are very tiny blood vessels that connect arteries and veins. Capillaries carry blood, oxygen, and nutrients to the body cells.

carbon dioxide page 14
When cells use nutrients and oxygen, they make a gas called carbon dioxide. Carbon dioxide leaves the body when you breathe out.

cardiogram page 138
A cardiogram is a record on paper of a person's heartbeat.

cerebellum page 29
Your cerebellum is the part of the brain that controls the way your body moves.

cerebrum page 28
Your cerebrum is the part of the brain that controls thinking, talking, and learning.

Cesarean section page 58
A Cesarean section is an operation that might be done if a mother is having trouble delivering her baby.

chemotherapy page 134
Chemotherapy is the treatment of cancer with powerful medicines.

child abusers page 66
Child abusers are people who hurt children in ways that are not accidents.

chlamydia page 116
Chlamydia is an STD that is caused by bacteria.

cholesterol page 125
Cholesterol is a fatty substance found in the blood. It can build up inside arteries and cause heart disease.

circulatory system page 13
Your circulatory system is the group of body parts that sends blood through your body.

clinics page 89
Clinics are places where doctors and nurses treat health problems.

cocaine page 85
Cocaine is an illegal drug that speeds up the nervous system. Its effects last a short time.

codeine page 84
Codeine is a prescription drug that reduces pain.

communicable diseases page 108
Communicable diseases can spread from one person to another.

communication page 43
Communication is sharing your thoughts or feelings with others.

compromise page 67
To compromise means to reach an agreement by having each side give up some of its demands.

confidential page 120
Confidential means secret.

counseling page 68
Counseling is giving advice and sharing ideas in order to help people solve their problems.

crack page 85
Crack is a strong form of cocaine. People smoke crack.

dependence page 77
Dependence is the very strong need for drugs.

depressant page 93
A depressant is a drug that slows down the nervous system.

diabetes page 128
Diabetes is a disease that prevents the body from using sugar in normal ways.

diagnosis page 137
A diagnosis is the name given to a disease or health condition. A doctor makes a diagnosis after examining and studying the symptoms of a patient.

digestion page 12
Digestion is the way the body breaks down your food into nutrients the body can use.

digestive system page 12
The digestive system is the group of organs that works together to break down food.

discharge page 116
Discharge comes out of an infected part of the body.

donor page 139
A donor is the person from whom body parts are taken to use in a transplant. A donor can be dead or living.

doses page 84
Doses are amounts of medicine that a person takes at one time.

drug abuse page 77
Drug abuse is using a drug in a way that is not correct. Drug abuse is also using a drug for no medical reason.

emotional health page 36
Emotional health is the way you live with your feelings. Good emotional health means that you have good feelings about yourself.

endocrine system page 30
Your endocrine system makes chemicals that help your body work and grow properly.

environment page 60
The environment includes the people, places, and objects that are around a person.

enzymes page 12
Enzymes are chemicals made by the body and used to break down food.

expiration date page 76
The expiration date is the last date that you should use a medicine.

extended family page 37
An extended family has one or both parents, one or more children, and other family members living in a home.

Fallopian tubes page 52
The egg cell travels through one of the Fallopian tubes as it leaves an ovary.

fertilized egg page 56
A fertilized egg is one that has joined with a sperm and can grow into a baby.

fiber page 128
Fiber is a nutrient from plant foods that helps the body remove wastes. Fiber is not digested and used by the body cells.

fibers page 28
Thin, threadlike parts attached to nerve cells are nerve fibers.

foster family page 37
A foster family is a family where adults care for one or more children because the children's natural parents cannot care for them.

glands page 30
The glands are parts of the body that make chemicals needed by the body.

hallucinogens page 86
Hallucinogens are drugs that change the way people see, hear, smell, taste, and feel.

heroin page 75
Heroin is a dangerous, habit-forming drug.

high page 78
To feel high means to have a good feeling that lasts a short time. People sometimes get high from abusing drugs.

HIV page 118
HIV is the virus that causes AIDS.

hormones page 30
Hormones are made by endocrine glands to help the body grow or stay healthy. Hormones enter the blood. The blood carries the hormones to the parts of the body where they are needed.

immune system page 110
The immune system includes different kinds of white blood cells and antibodies that work together to fight disease.

immunity page 110
Immunity means the body can fight off a disease without becoming sick.

infections page 23
Infections are caused by germs growing in all or part of the body.

inhalants page 87
People sniff inhalants in order to have pleasant feelings.

inherited page 60
Inherited means a person received certain traits from his or her parents.

insulin page 128
Insulin is a hormone that helps the body digest sugar.

involuntary muscles page 7
Involuntary muscles receive messages from the brain so they can work on their own to control many organs of the body.

joints page 6
Joints are places where bones meet.

kidneys page 23
The kidneys are a pair of organs that removes liquid waste from the blood.

labor page 57
Labor is the physical work done by a female's body to give birth to a baby.

large intestine page 13
The large intestine stores solid waste until the solid waste leaves the body.

latex page 121
Latex is a strong, stretchy material like rubber.

leukemia page 131
Leukemia causes the body to make too many white blood cells that are not normal. These white blood cells cannot fight germs.

life cycle page 56
The life cycle is the five stages of life from birth until death.

mammogram page 138
A mammogram is an x-ray picture of a breast.

marijuana page 84
Marijuana is an illegal drug that people use to feel high.

mature page 50
Mature describes something or someone that is fully grown or fully developed.

medulla page 29
The medulla is the part of the brain that controls the body's systems.

menstruation page 52
Menstruation is the three-to-seven-day period when the egg cell flows out of the uterus with some blood.

mole page 133
A mole is a black or brown spot on the skin.

narcotic page 84
A narcotic is a drug that reduces pain and causes dependence.

natural parent page 37
A natural parent is related to the child by blood.

nervous system page 28
Your nervous system controls your thinking and the way your body moves and works.

nicotine page 100
Nicotine is a drug in tobacco that causes dependence.

noncommunicable disease page 124
A noncommunicable disease does not spread from one person to another. It is not caused by pathogens.

nutrients page 11
Nutrients are substances in food that the body needs for health and life.

opposite sex page 45
The opposite sex is the one that is different from your own. If you are a male, a member of the opposite sex is a female.

organs page 5
Organs are made of large groups of cells. Each body organ has a certain job to do.

osteoporosis page 8
Osteoporosis is a bone disease in which the bones become thinner and break easily.

ovaries page 52
Ovaries are female sex glands that produce female hormones and egg cells.

oxygen page 5
Oxygen is a gas that has no color or smell.

Pap test page 134
A Pap test checks for cancer in a female's reproductive organs.

passive smoker page 101
A passive smoker breathes smoke from the cigarettes, pipes, or cigars of other people.

pathogens page 109
Pathogens are very tiny living things that cause disease. They are too small to be seen without a microscope.

peer pressure page 65
Peer pressure is the control over your decisions that people your age try to have.

perspiration page 22
Perspiration is a liquid that is made by the body. It contains water, salt, and wastes from your blood.

physical health page 31
Physical health is how you take care of your body. Eating healthy foods, exercising, and sleeping enough are ways to take care of your physical health.

pierce page 121
Pierce means to make a hole in something. Many people pierce their ears and wear earrings in the holes.

pituitary gland page 30
The pituitary gland makes hormones that control other endocrine glands as well as the growth of the bones.

pneumonia page 116
Pneumonia is an infection of the lungs.

polluted page 21
Polluted describes something that is dirty and unhealthy.

posture page 7
Your posture is the way you carry your body when you stand, sit, and move.

pregnancy page 46
Pregnancy is having one or more unborn children growing inside a female's body.

pressure page 65
Pressure is a strong demand.

puberty page 49
Puberty is the time when the sex organs and the sex glands begin to work.

radiation page 134
Radiation is a treatment for cancer. Very strong rays are aimed at cancer cells to kill them.

recovering alcoholics page 96
Recovering alcoholics have learned how to stop drinking alcohol.

rejection page 140
Rejection happens when the immune system attacks the organ a person receives during a transplant. People can die from organ rejection.

relationships page 42
Relationships are the way you get along with others.

reproduce page 109
To reproduce means to make other living things. People reproduce by having babies. Bacteria make more bacteria when they reproduce.

reproductive organs page 50
Reproductive organs are the parts of the body that allow males and females to produce children.

respiratory system page 19
Your respiratory system is a group of organs that work for the body to take in oxygen and give off carbon dioxide.

responsibilities page 38
Responsibilities are jobs you do that show you can be trusted to do things well.

risk behaviors page 46
Risk behaviors are behaviors that can harm your health.

scoliosis page 7
Scoliosis is an unhealthy curving of the spine.

self-esteem page 38
Self-esteem is the good feelings you have about yourself.

sexual page 45
Sexual describes anything that has to do with being a male or a female.

sexually transmitted diseases
page 46
Sexually transmitted diseases are diseases that can be spread from person to person through intimate sexual behavior.

side effects page 76
Side effects are unpleasant and sometimes dangerous effects medicines have on the body.

sidestream smoke page 101
Sidestream smoke is the smoke sent into the air by the burning end of a cigarette, pipe, or cigar.

small intestine page 12
The small intestine is a long tube where most of the digestion of food is finished.

smokeless tobacco page 100
Smokeless tobacco is made from tobacco leaves and is chewed, dipped, or sniffed.

social health page 36
Social health is the way you get along with others. Good social health means you try to get along with your family and friends.

sperm cells page 51
Sperm cells are male reproductive cells.

SPF page 132
SPF stands for sun protection factor. An SPF number tells how much protection a sunscreen provides.

spinal cord page 28
Your spinal cord is a thick row of nerves that goes down the center of your back.

stimulants page 85
Stimulants are drugs that speed up the body's systems.

strep bacteria page 111
Strep bacteria cause sore throats and other diseases.

stress page 31
Stress is the way the body responds to different kinds of demands.

stroke page 125
A stroke is a disease that damages the brain. It happens when blood cannot flow through a blocked artery to the brain.

sunscreen lotion page 132
A sunscreen lotion blocks the sun's harmful rays from damaging your skin.

surgery page 134
Surgery is the use of medical tools to cut and repair the body.

symptoms page 116
Symptoms are signs of a disease.

systems page 5
Systems are groups of organs that work together to do different jobs for the body.

testes page 51
The testes are the male endocrine glands that make male sex hormones.

throat culture page 111
A throat culture is the growth of bacteria from the throat. The bacteria grow in a small, closed dish. A throat culture helps a doctor learn what kind of pathogen is causing a person's sore throat.

thyroid gland page 31
The thyroid gland makes a hormone that controls the speed with which the body uses food.

tolerance page 78
Tolerance means the body needs more of a drug to get the same feeling it once felt with smaller amounts.

traditional family page 37
A traditional family has a mother, a father, and one or more children.

traits page 60
Traits are characteristics, such as skin and eye color, that belong to each person.

tranquilizers page 84
Tranquilizers are prescription drugs that have a calming effect because they slow down the nervous system.

transplants page 139
Transplants are body parts from a healthy person that replace the diseased parts of another person.

tumor page 132
A tumor is a lump that grows in the body. A tumor can be made of normal cells or cancer cells.

ultrasound page 138
Ultrasound is the use of sound waves to outline the shape of a person's body parts.

umbilical cord page 57
The umbilical cord is a thick cord made of blood vessels that connects the baby's navel to its mother's uterus.

urinary system page 19
Your urinary system is a group of organs that removes liquid waste from the body.

urinate page 23
To urinate is to rid the body of urine.

urine page 23
Urine is the liquid waste that is made by the kidneys.

uterus page 52
The uterus is the female organ where a developing baby grows during pregnancy.

vaccines page 110
Vaccines are medicines that help the body make antibodies. Vaccines protect you from getting certain diseases.

vagina page 57
The vagina is the part of a female's body that goes from the uterus to outside the body.

values page 38
Your values are your ideas about what is important.

veins page 13
Veins are blood vessels that carry blood from other parts of the body back to the heart.

virus page 108
A virus is a very tiny living thing that causes disease. A virus can multiply and grow only when it is inside the body's cells.

voluntary muscles page 6
You can control voluntary muscles in order to move your body.

wellness page 46
Wellness means having good physical, social, and emotional health. Wellness is the highest health goal.

withdrawal page 85
Withdrawal is the body's painful reaction to not having a drug on which it is dependent.

Chart: Drugs Used in Substance Abuse

Drug Group	Drug	What do people call it?	Can people buy the drug legally?	How do people get the drug into their bodies?
Stimulants	cocaine	coke, snow	no	sniff it, inject it, smoke it
	crack	rock	no	smoke it
	amphetamines	speed, uppers, pep pills	yes, with a prescription	swallow pills, inject it
Hemp Plant	marijuana	pot, grass, dope	no	smoke it, eat it
Depressants	barbiturates	downers	yes, with a prescription	swallow pills
	tranquilizers	Valium, Librium	yes, with a prescription	swallow pills
	alcohol	booze	yes, if you have reached the legal age	swallow it

What happens right after a person uses the drug?	What effects might the drug have on a person who uses the drug for a long time?	What happens during withdrawal?
The person feels very high, then feels very sad; has a loss of appetite; has nervous feelings; has a fast heartbeat; has high blood pressure; or cannot sleep.	The person may have strong emotional dependence on the drug, develop tolerance for larger amounts of the drug, feel very sad when the drug wears off, have violent behavior, suffer heart attacks, or die.	The person may feel a very strong hunger for the drug or feel very tired and sad.
The person feels alert and full of energy, cannot sleep, experiences fast breathing and fast heartbeat, has a loss of appetite, or dies.	The person may have emotional dependence on the drug, have tolerance for larger amounts of the drug, have poor nutrition, have violent behavior, or suffer brain damage.	The person may feel very tired and sad.
The person feels high, cannot think or remember clearly, or has red eyes.	The person may have emotional dependence on the drug, have tolerance for larger amounts of the drug, suffer damage to the lungs, or have lung cancer.	unknown
The person feels sleepy, calm, and relaxed; has slow heartbeat and slow breathing; has stomachache; has poor memory; makes poor decisions; has poor speech; or feels dizzy.	The person may have emotional and physical dependence on the drug, feel very tired or sad, suffer damage to the body's systems, or overdose and die.	The person may be nervous, have body shakes, be unable to sleep, or die.

Chart: Drugs Used in Substance Abuse

Drug Group	Drug	What do people call it?	Can people buy the drug legally?	How do people get the drug into their bodies?
Narcotics	heroin	junk, horse	no	inject it, inhale it, smoke it
	methadone	Dolophine	yes, with a prescription	swallow it, inject it
	codeine	codeine in cough medicine or Tylenol with codeine	yes, with a prescription	swallow it
Inhalants	airplane glue gasoline shellac nail polish remover		Yes; inhalants are found in common household products.	inhale it
Hallucinogens	PCP	angel dust	no	swallow it, smoke it, inhale it, inject it
	LSD	acid	no	swallow it
	mescaline	mesc	no	swallow it, sometimes smoke it
Steroids	Anatrol Winstrol		yes, with a prescription	swallow it, inject it

What happens right after a person uses the drug?	What effects might the drug have on a person who uses the drug for a long time?	What happens during withdrawal?
The person feels no pain, feels sleepy, has happy and calm feelings, or has stomachache.	The person may have strong emotional and physical dependence on the drug, have tolerance for larger doses of the drug, or overdose and die.	The person may have fever, body shakes, sweating, chills, or vomiting. The person may die.
The person has poor body movements, has a cough, feels tired, is confused, or has slow heartbeat and slow breathing. At times the person may be unconscious.	The person may have emotional dependence on the drug; have violent behavior; suffer damage to the liver, brain, and blood cells; have tolerance for larger doses of the drug; or die.	unknown
The person imagines seeing and hearing beautiful or scary sights and sounds, has loss of appetite, or is nervous.	The person may have emotional dependence on the drug, have violent behavior, suffer lung damage or brain damage, have emotional problems, or have flashbacks.	unknown
The person builds body muscles quickly, gains weight quickly, or has acne.	The person may have violent behavior, feel very sad, and may suffer damage to the heart and the liver.	unknown